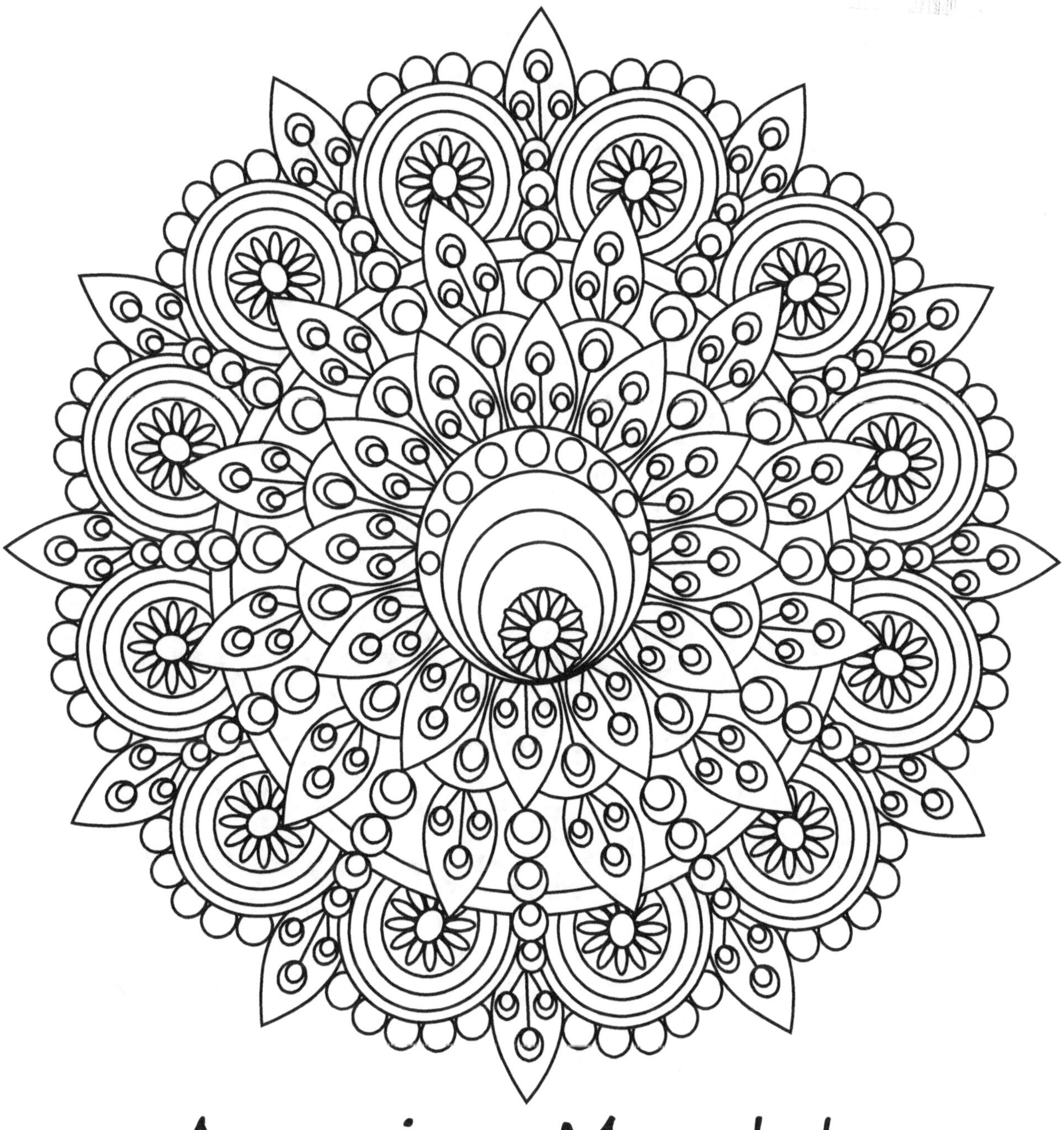

Amazing Mandalas

Coloring Book-Volume 2

Ruchi Bhargava

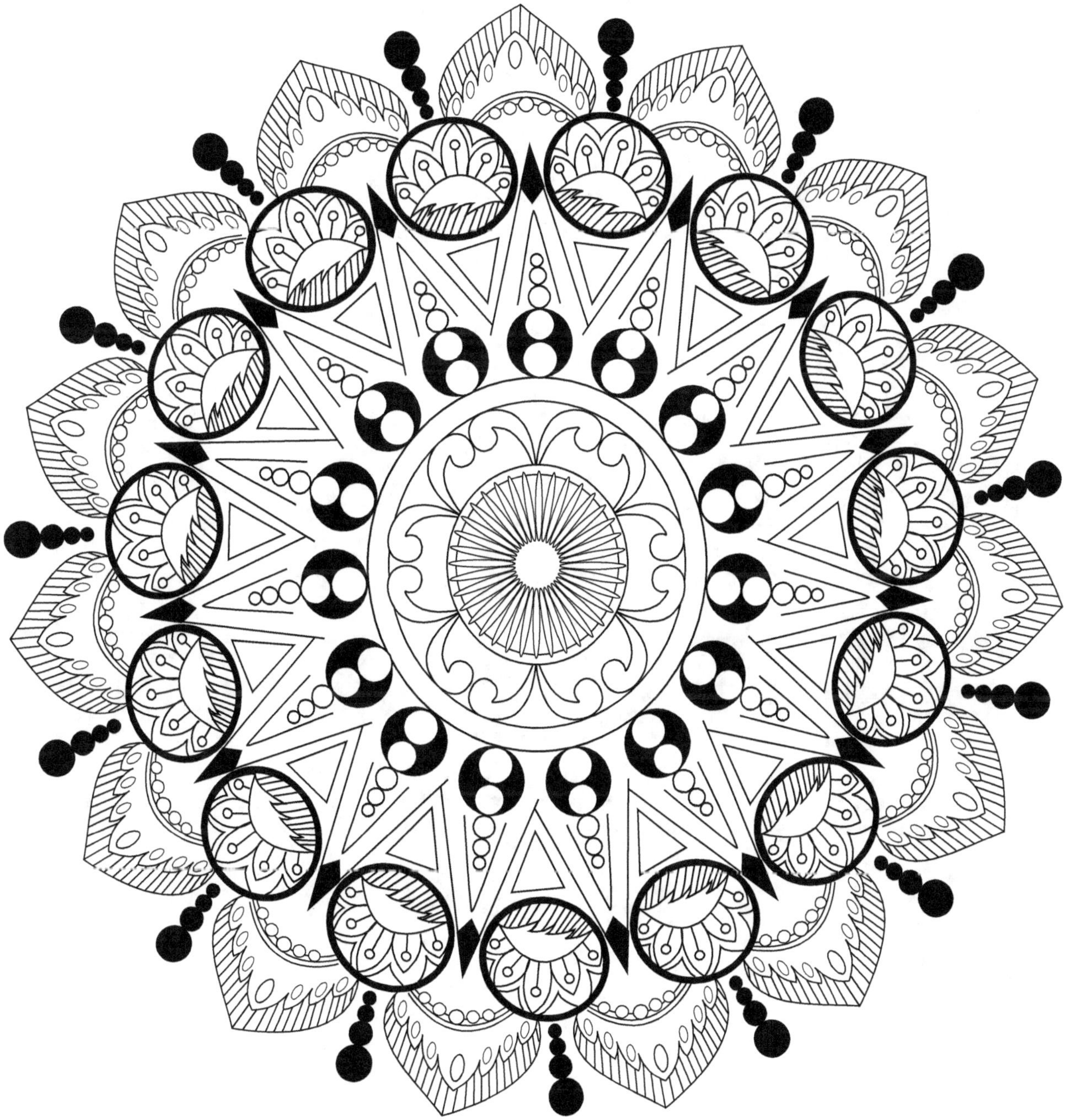

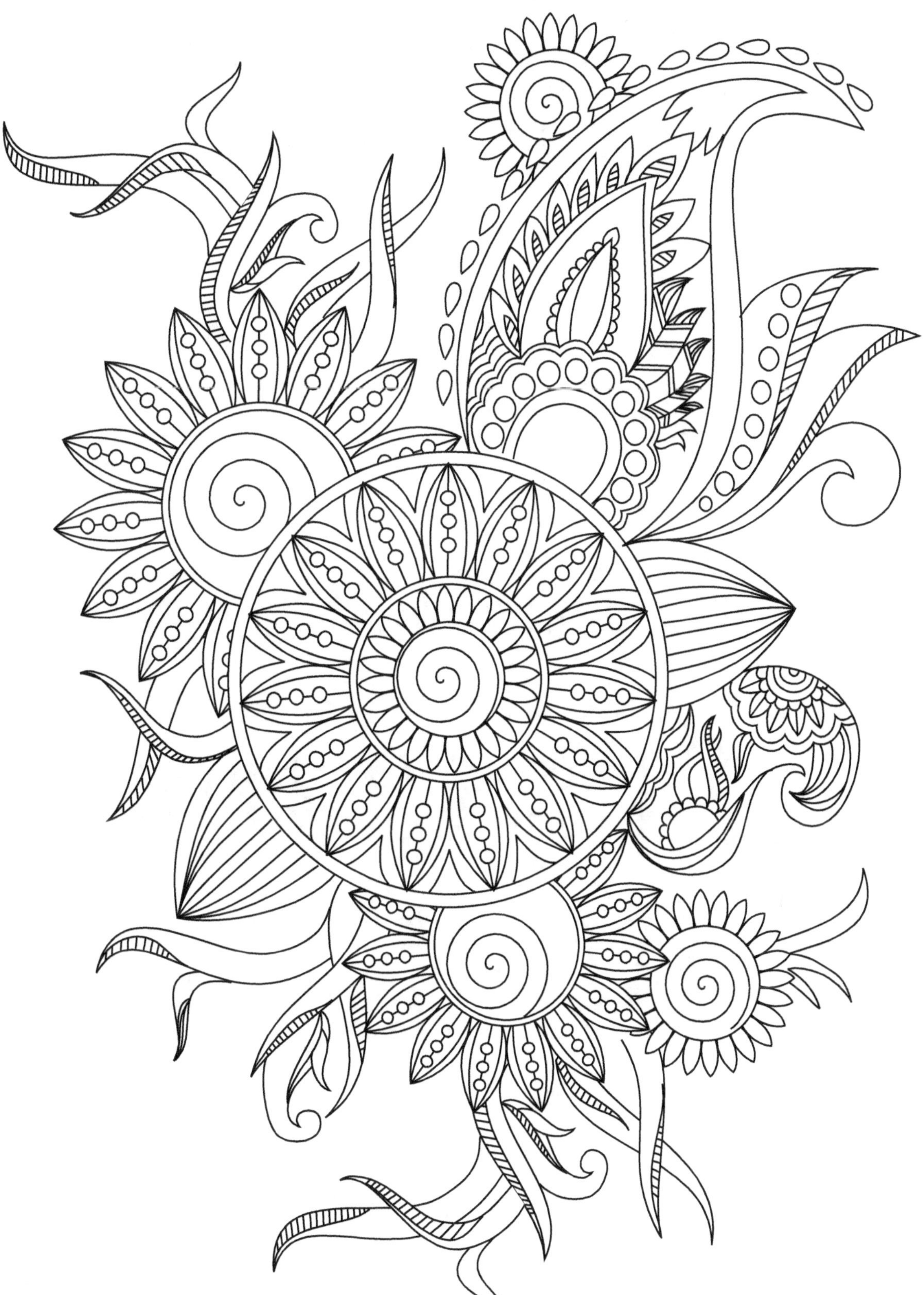

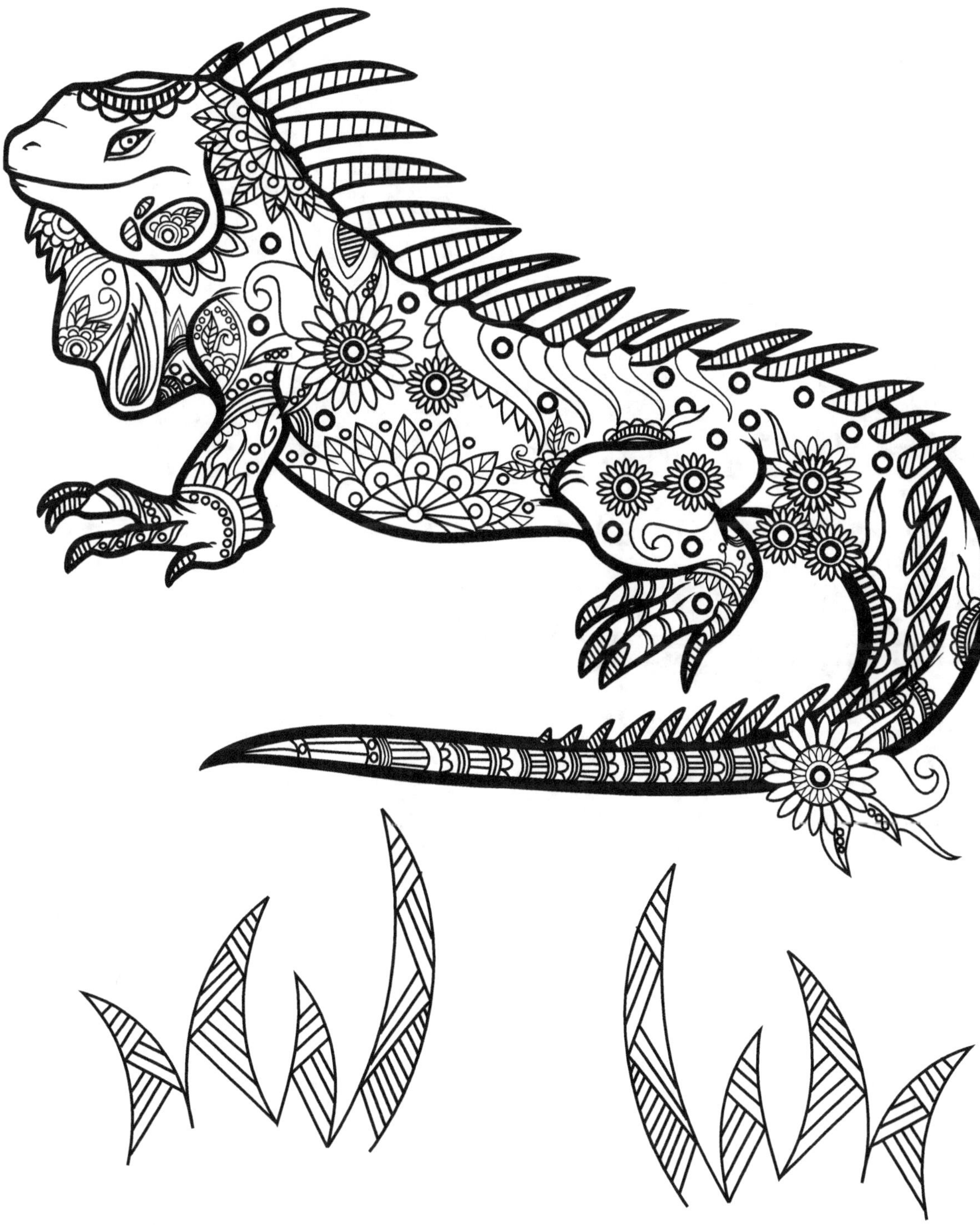

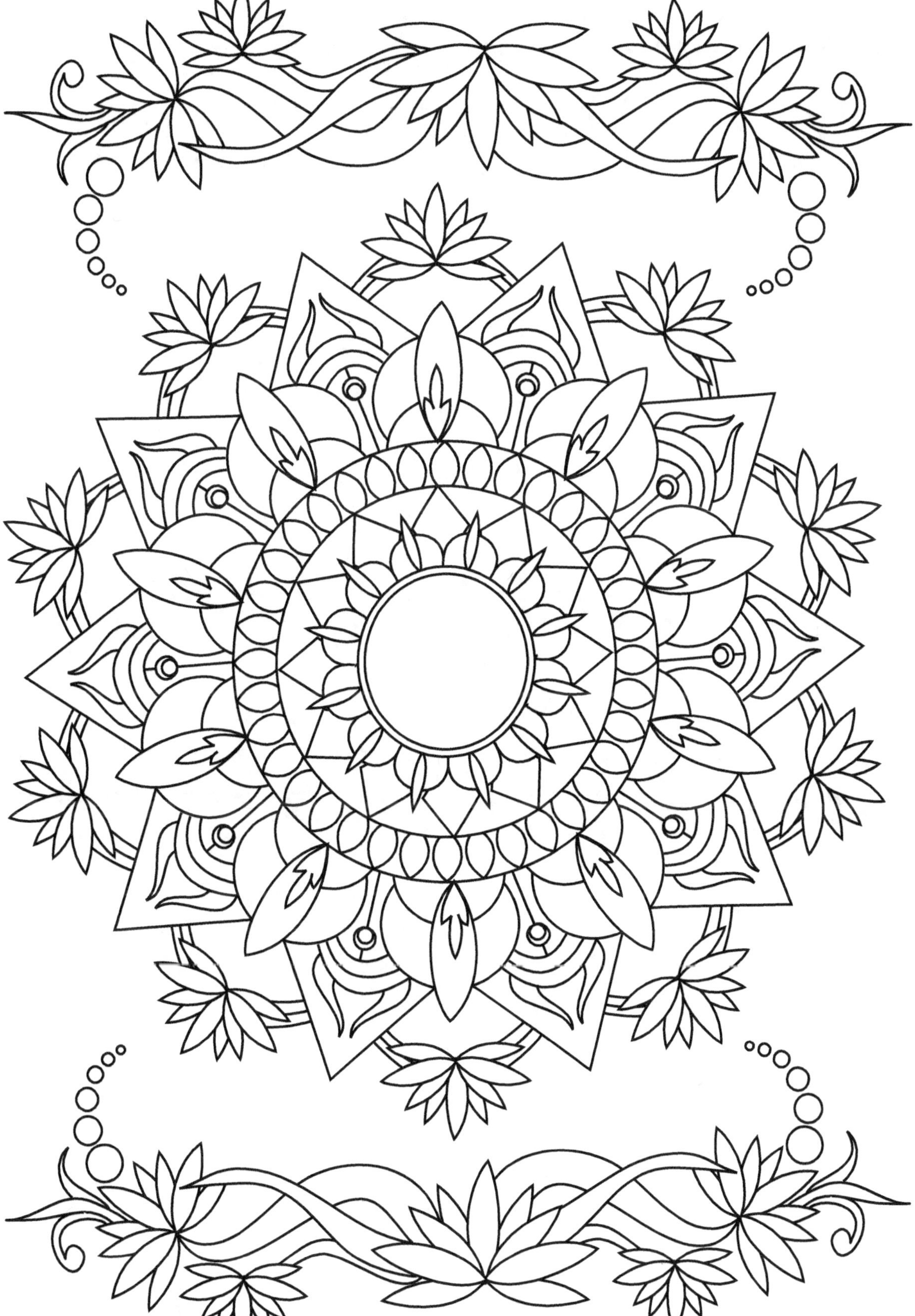

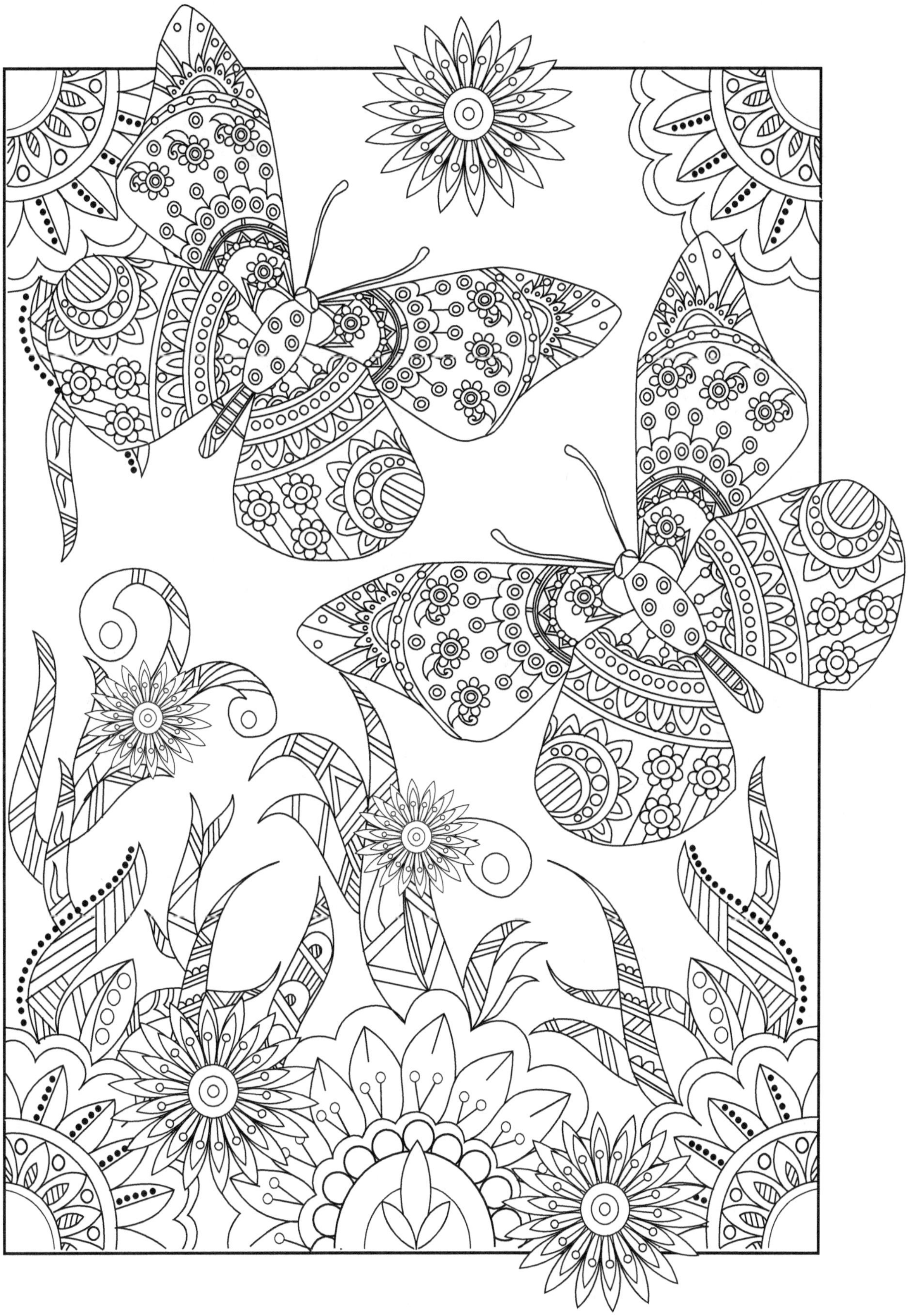

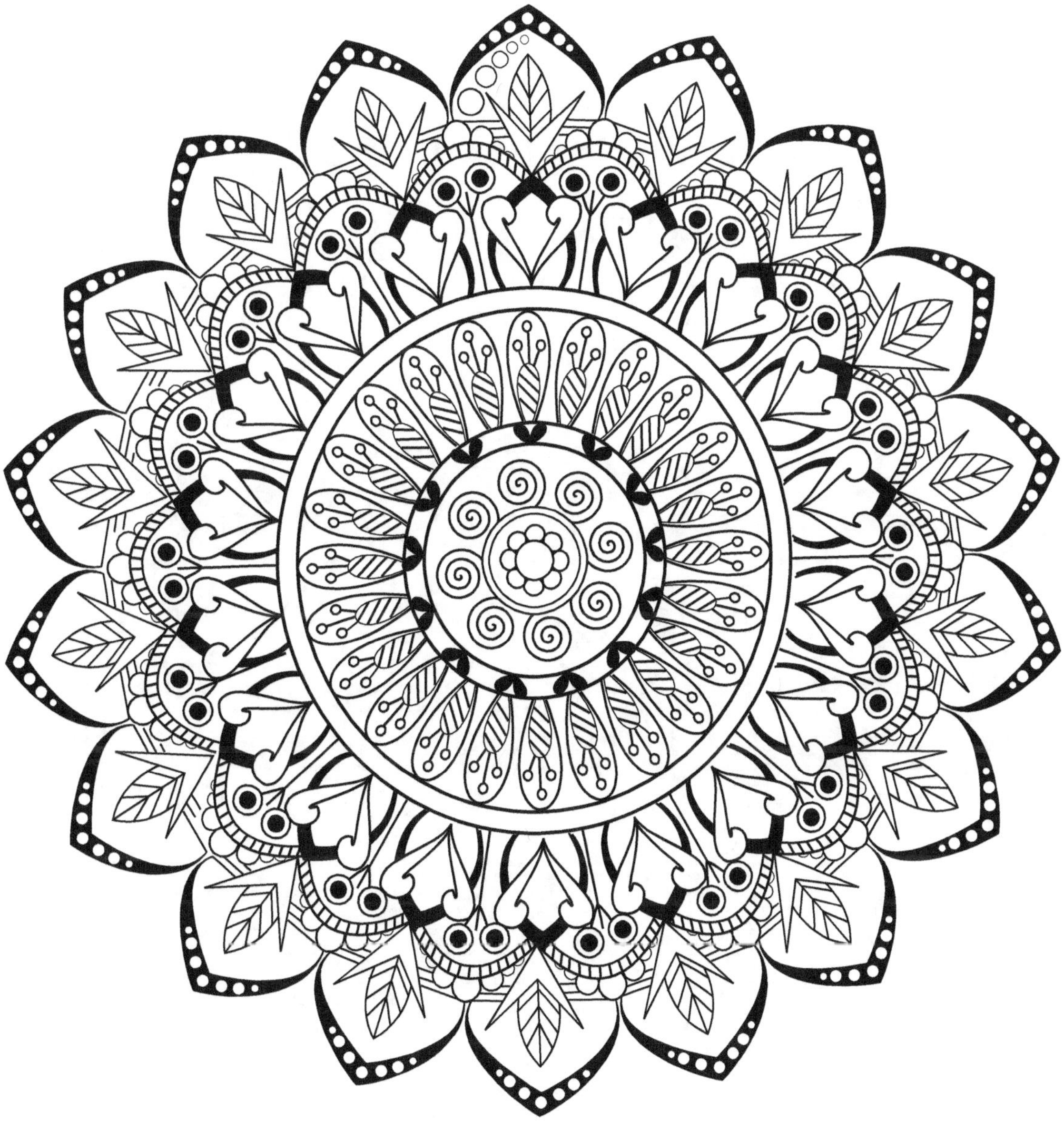

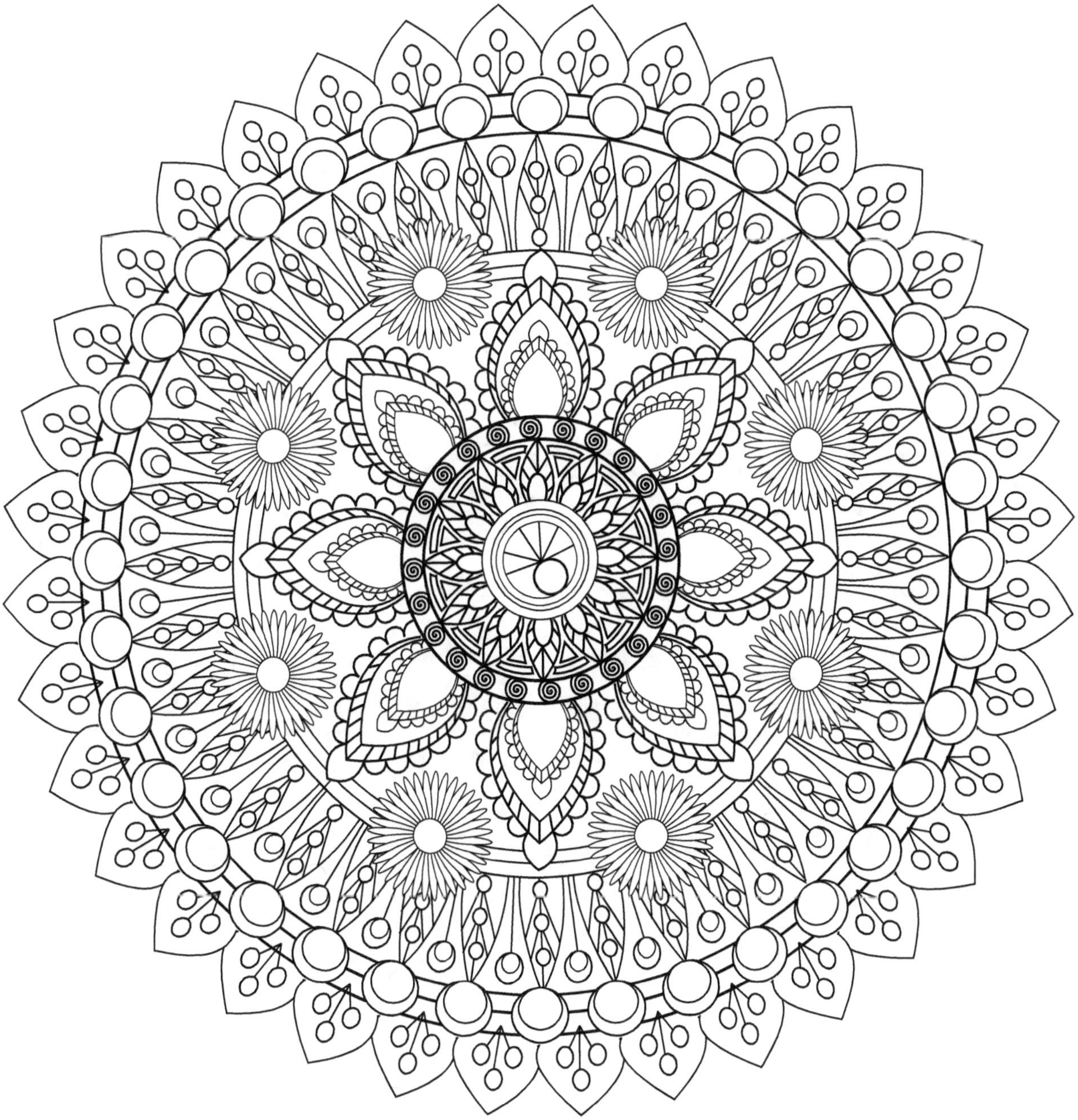

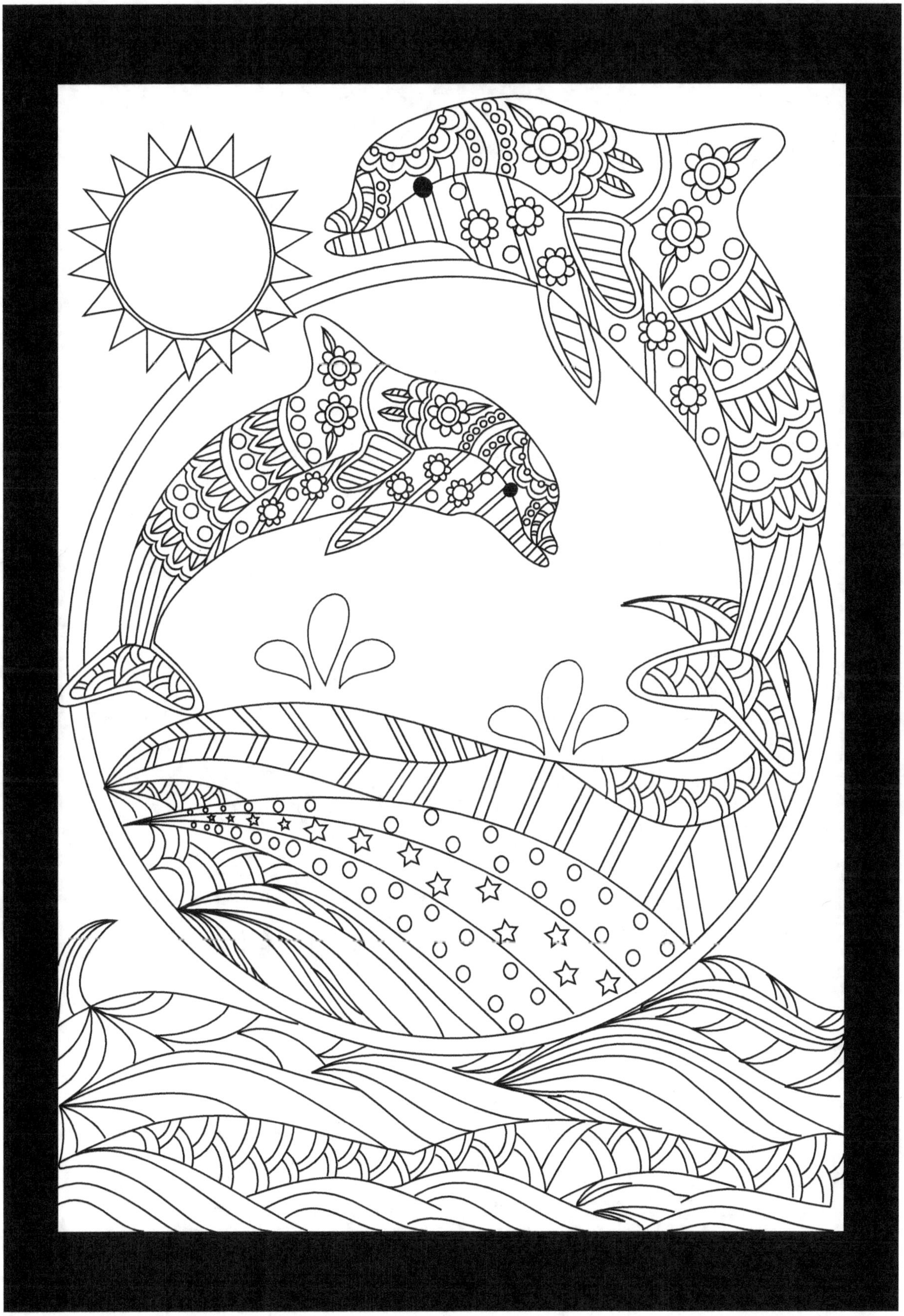

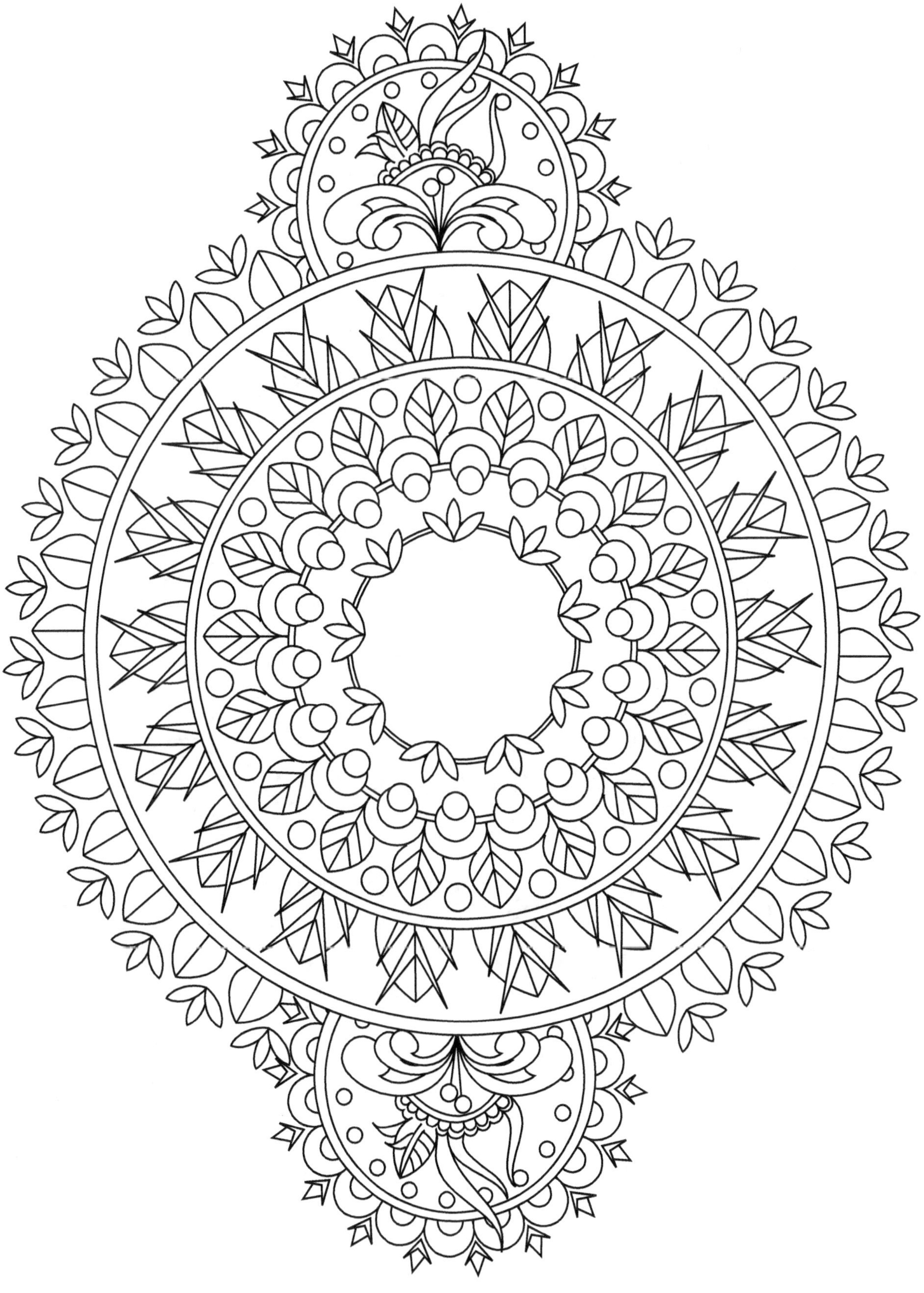

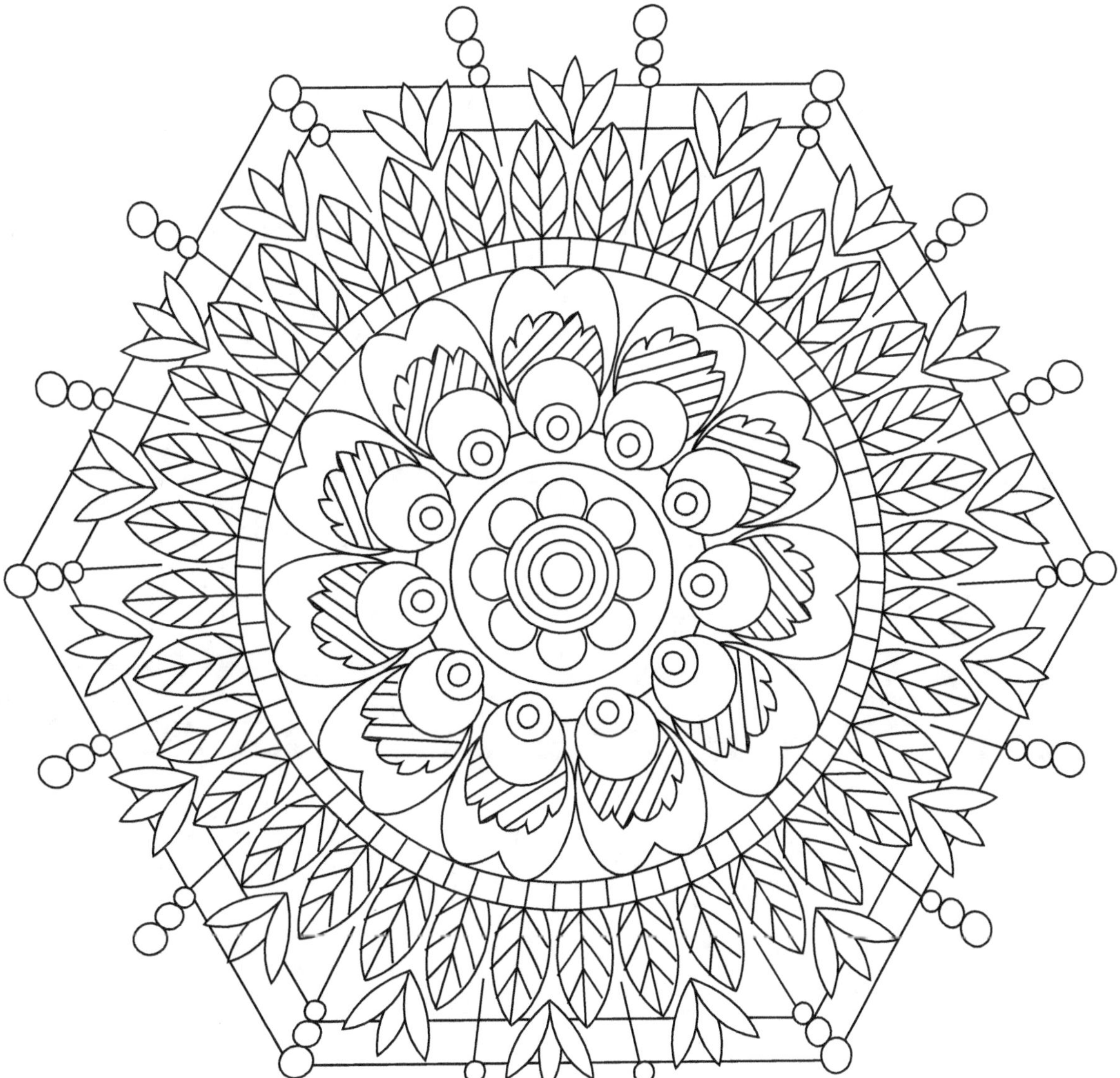

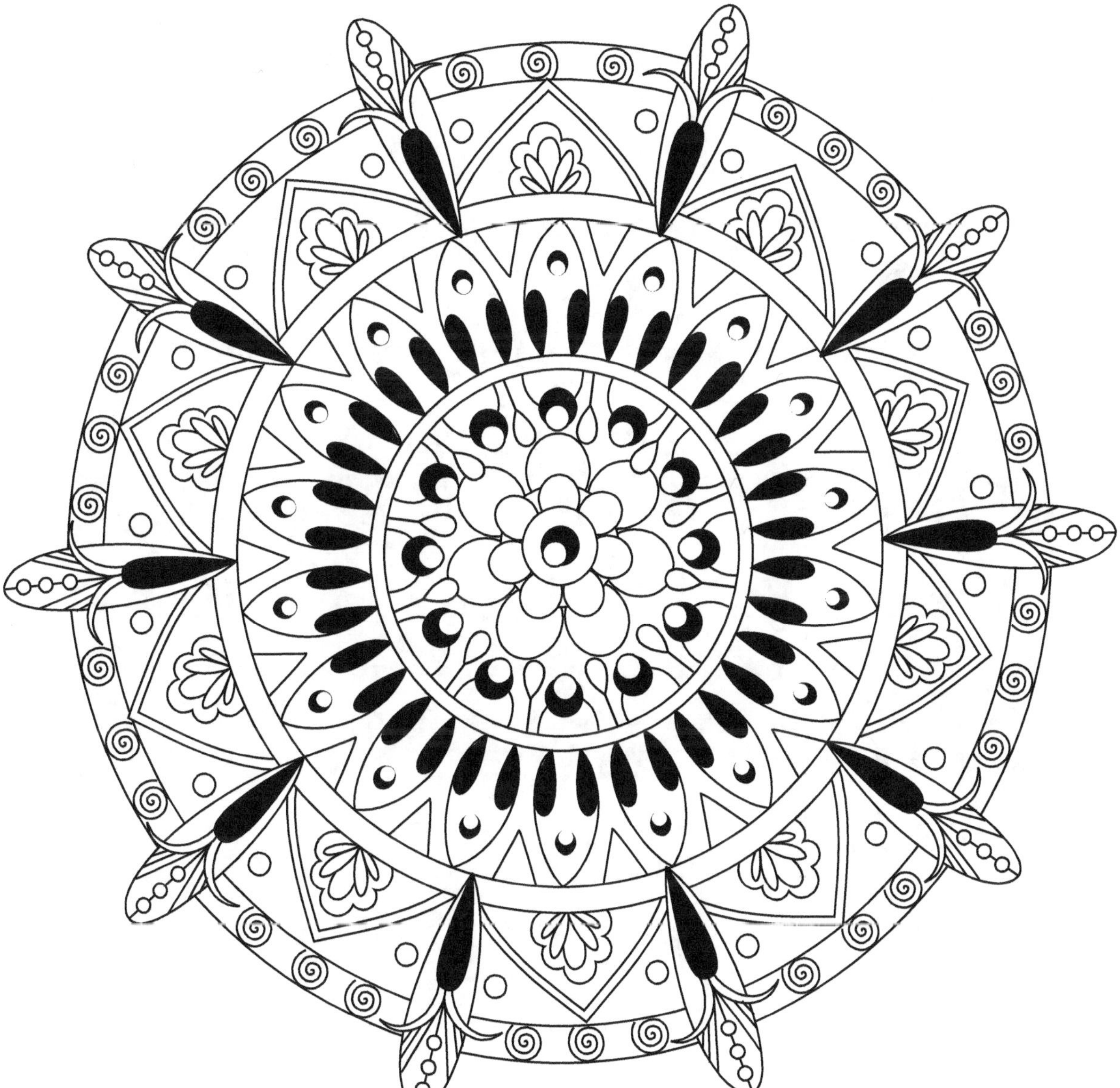

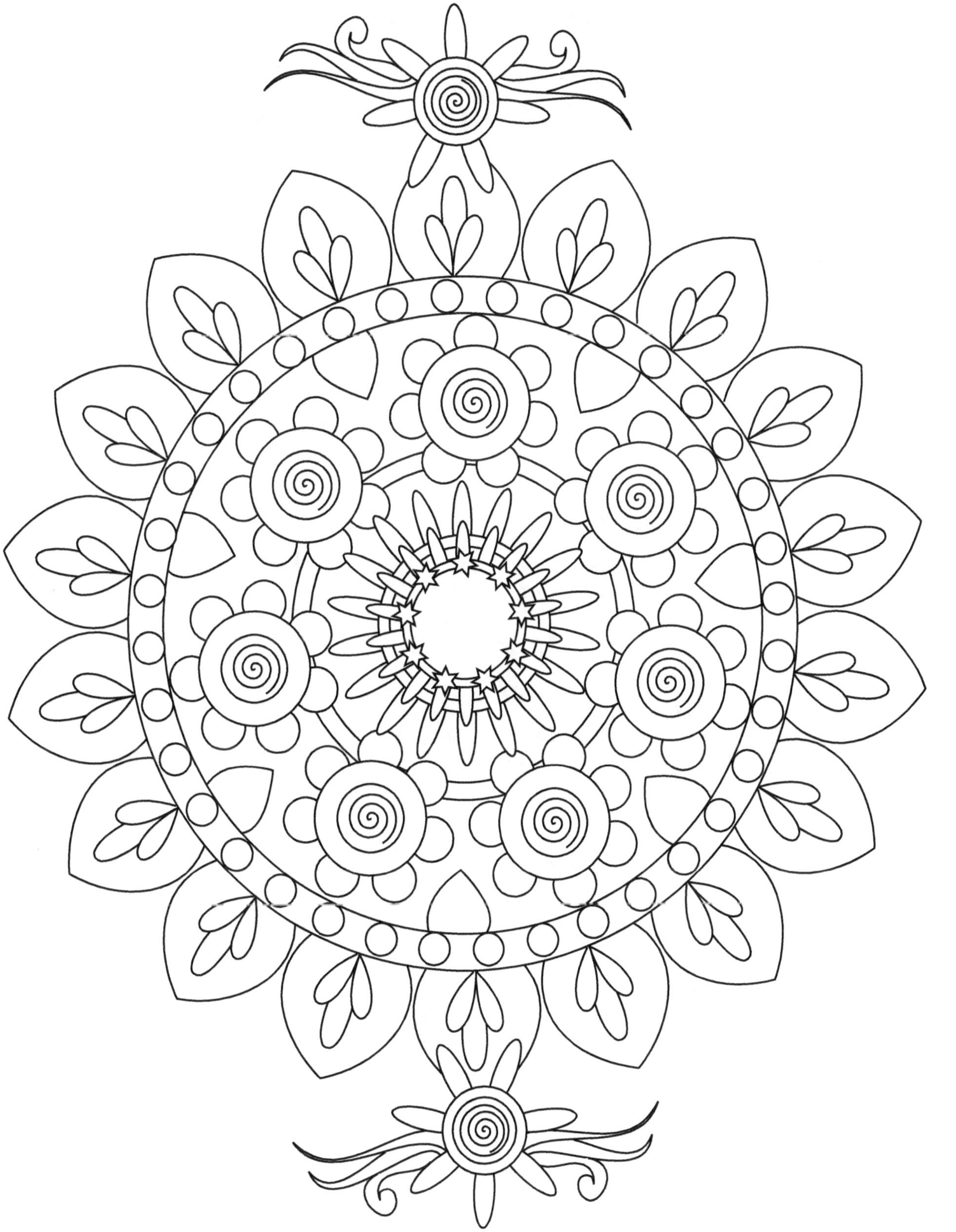

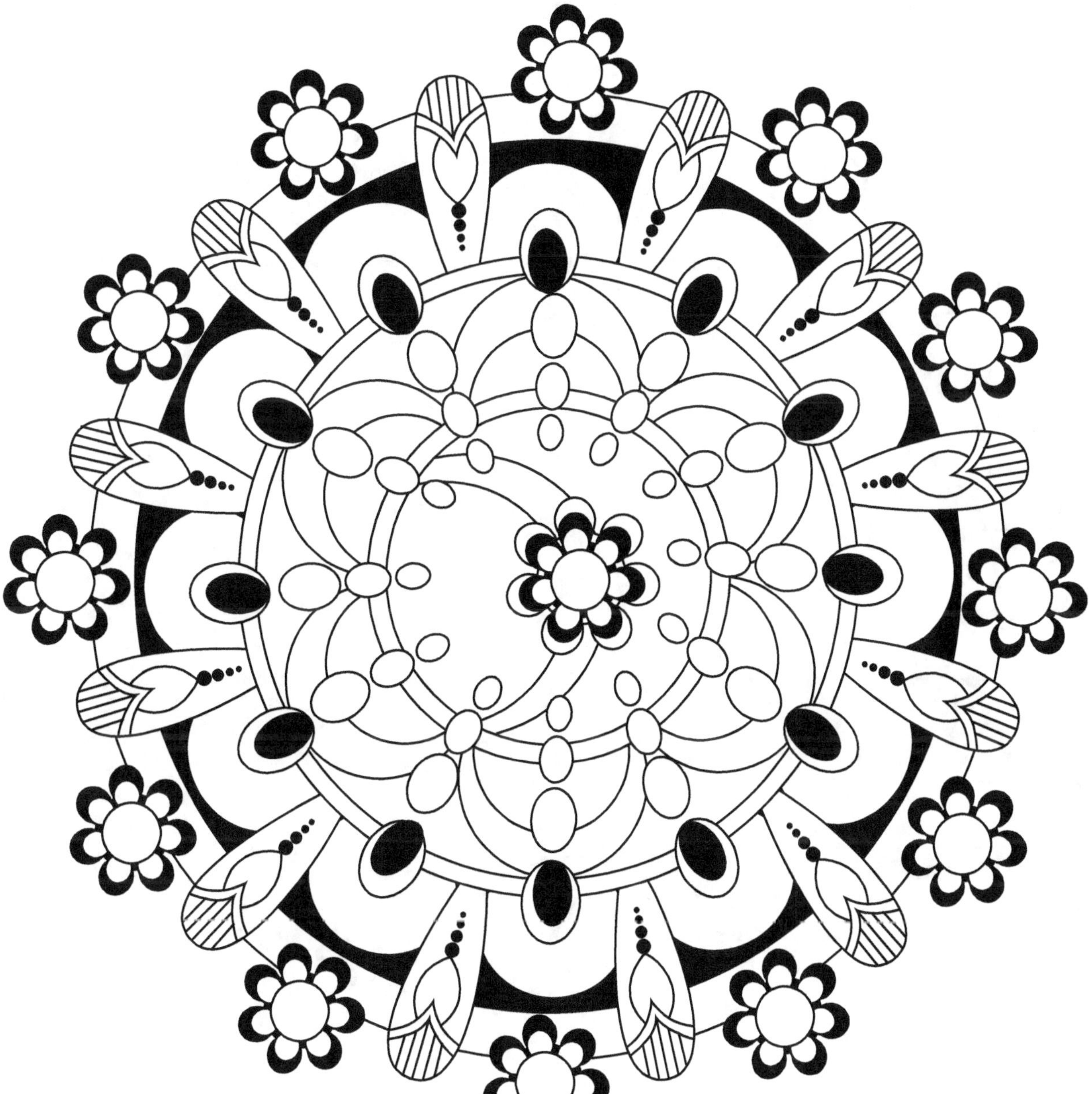

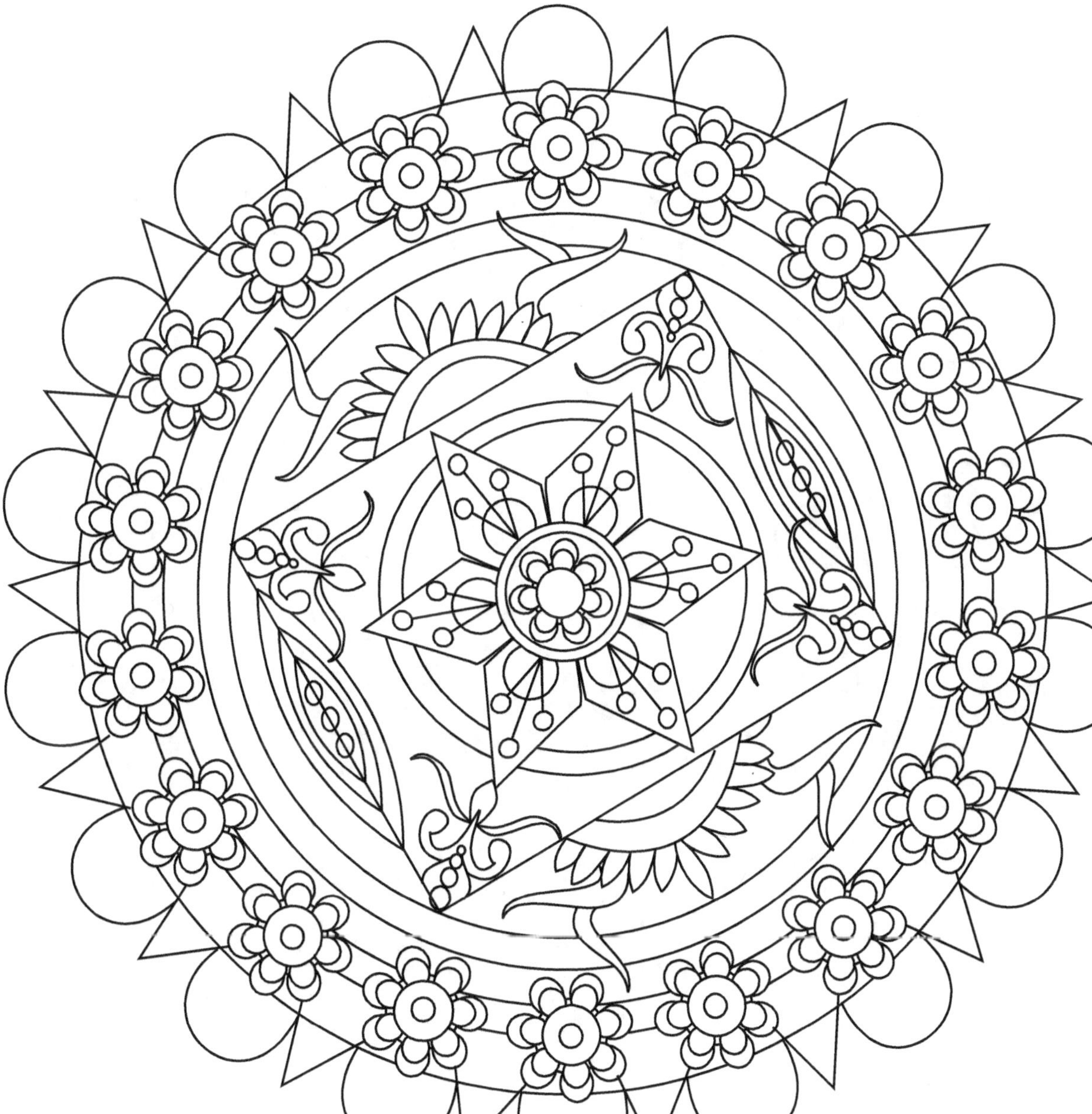

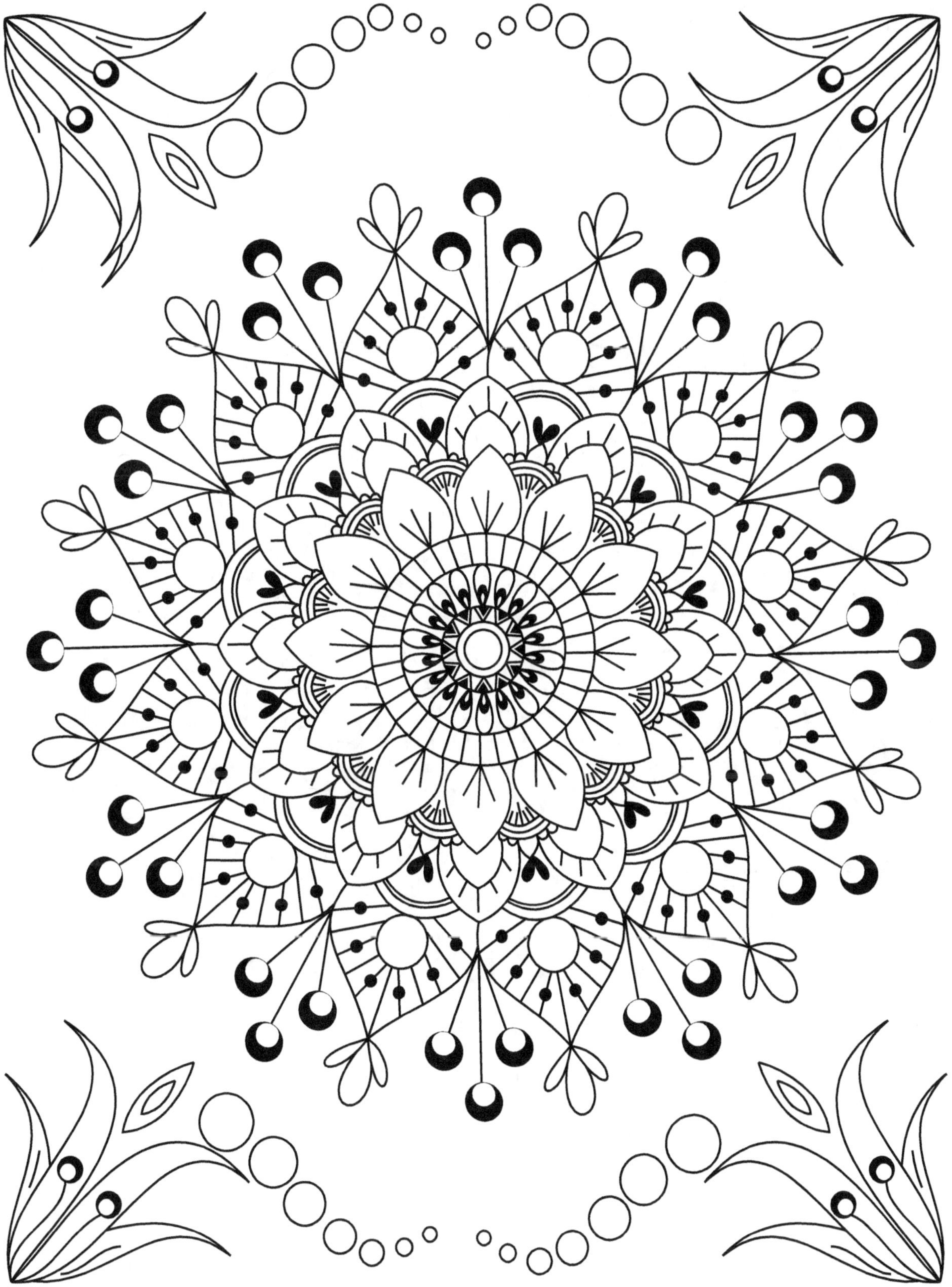

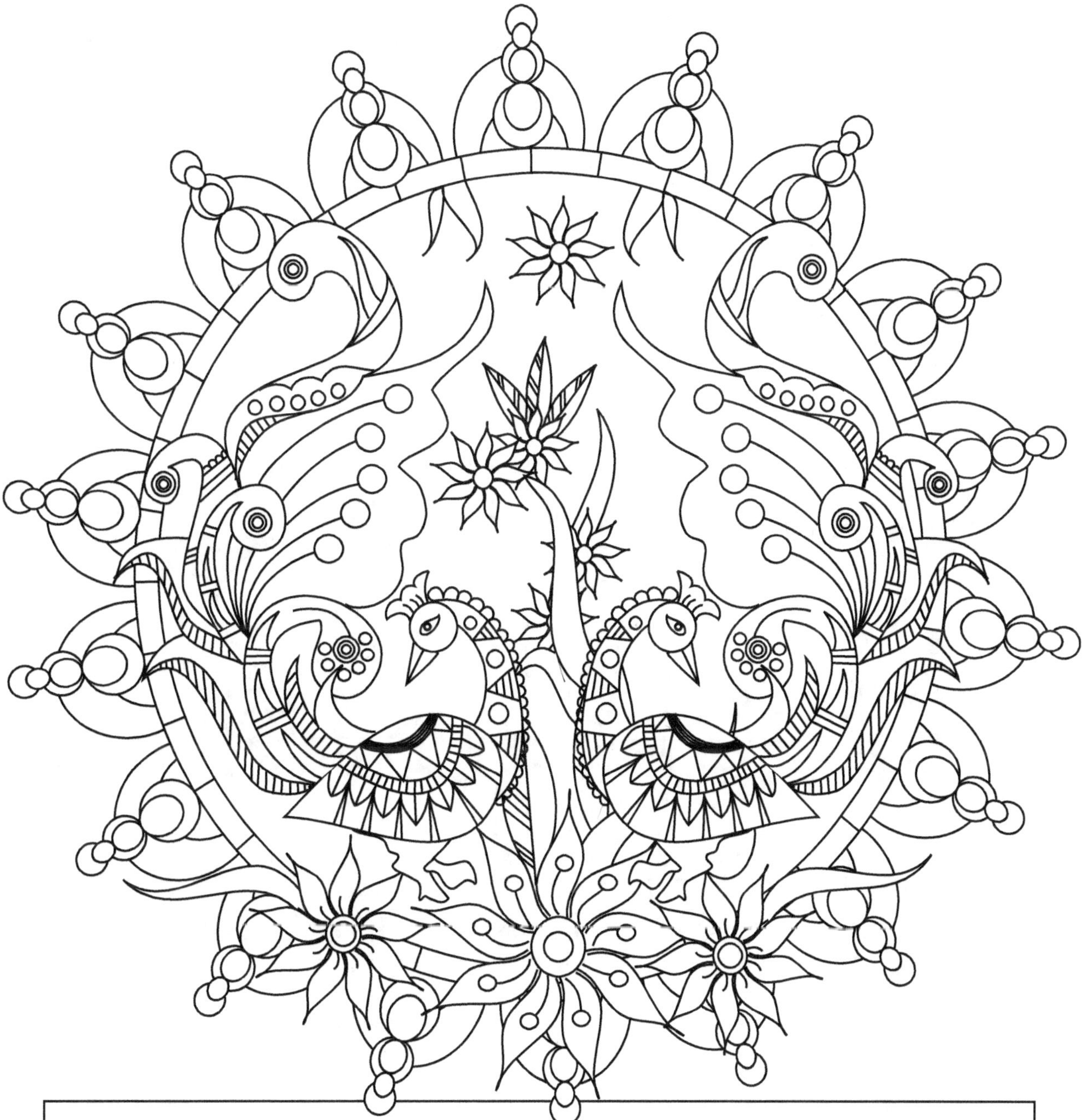

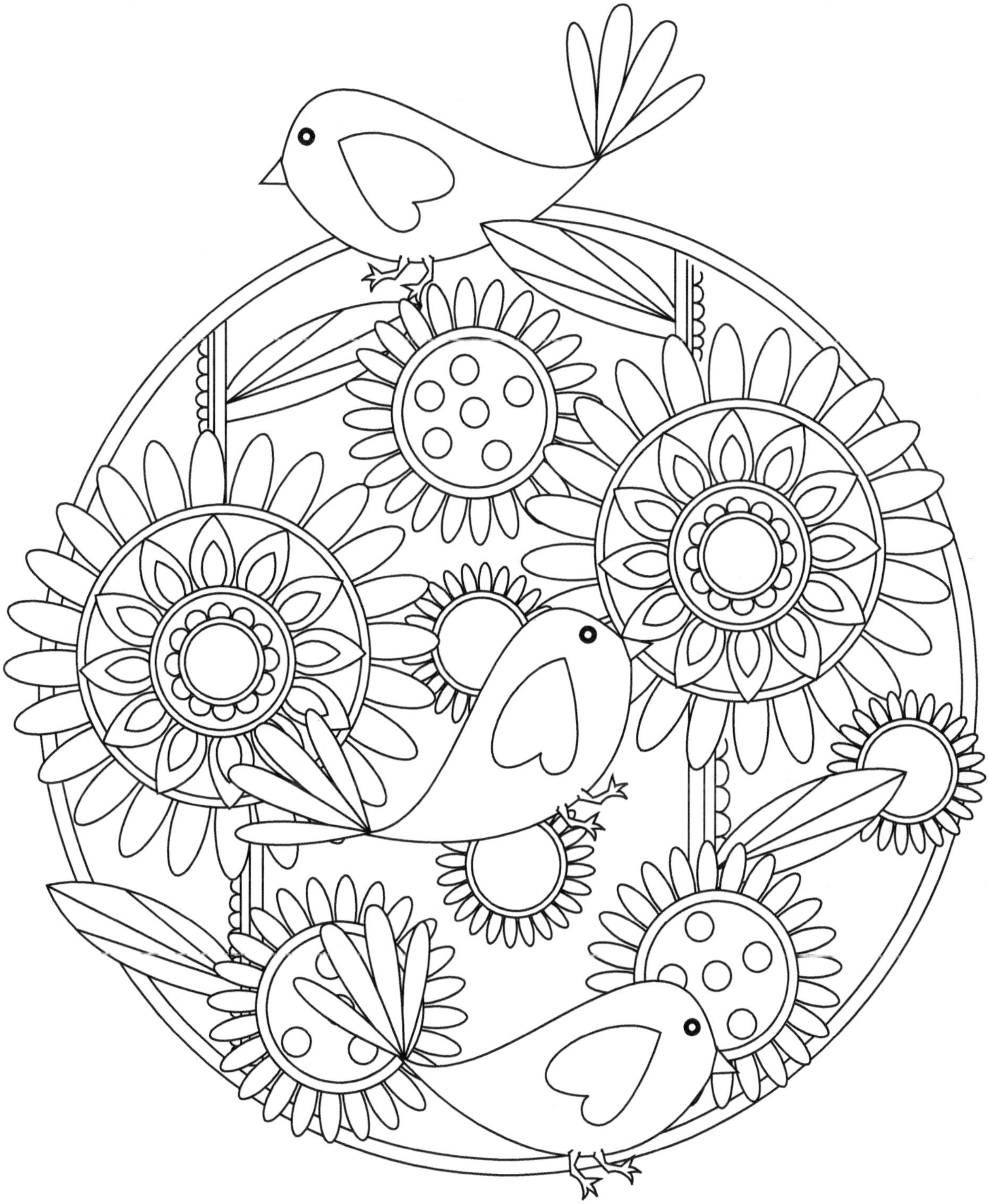

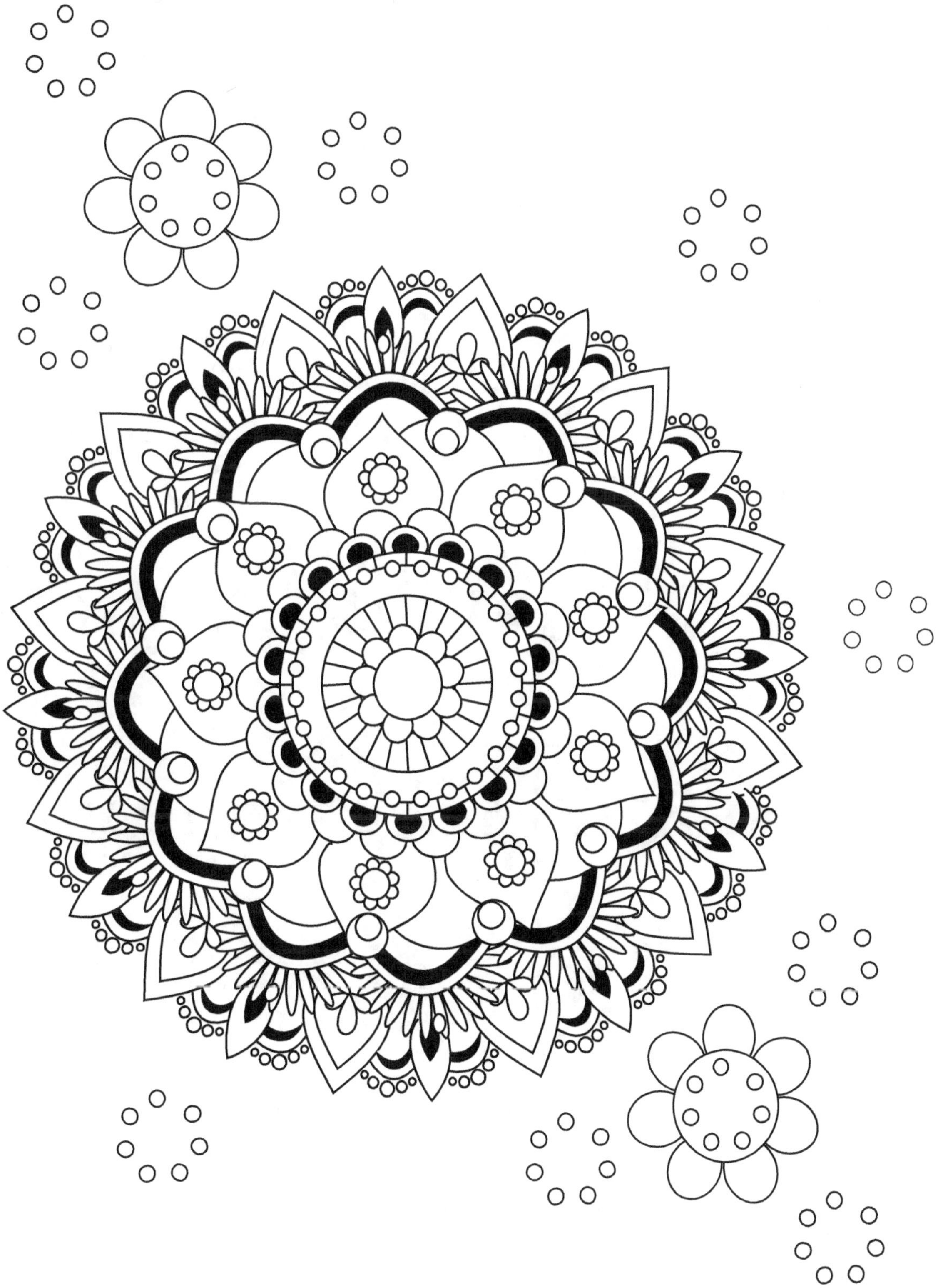

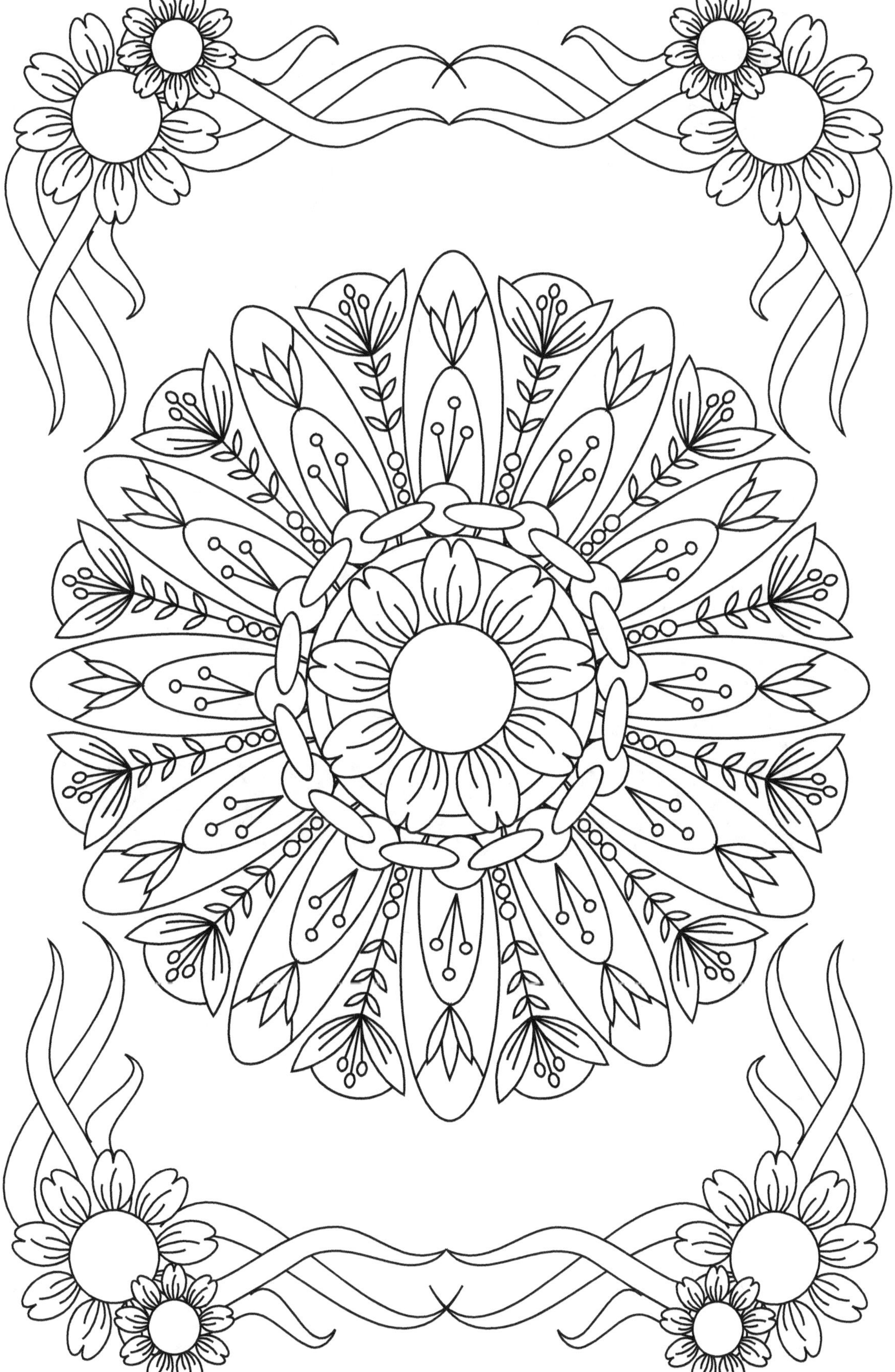

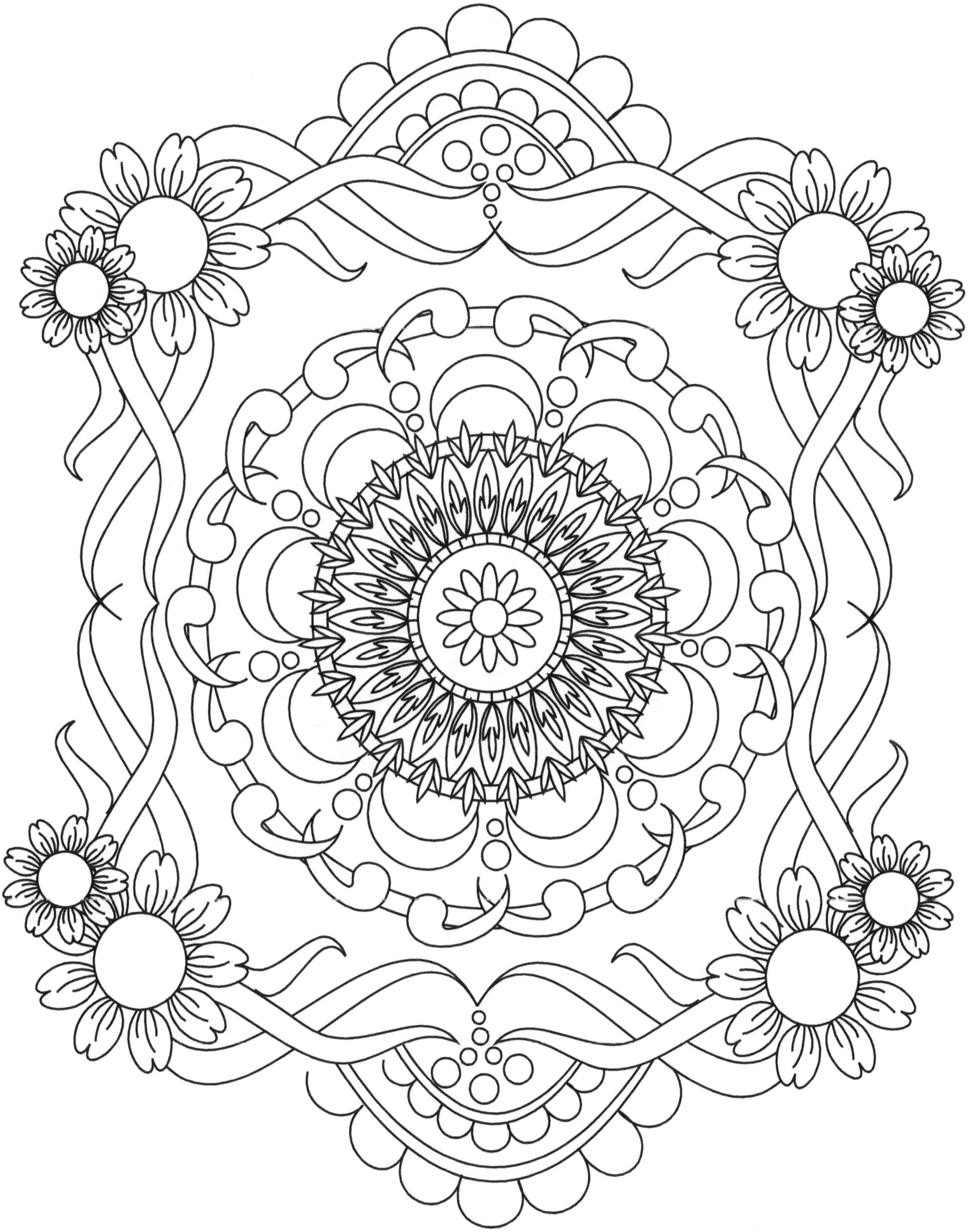

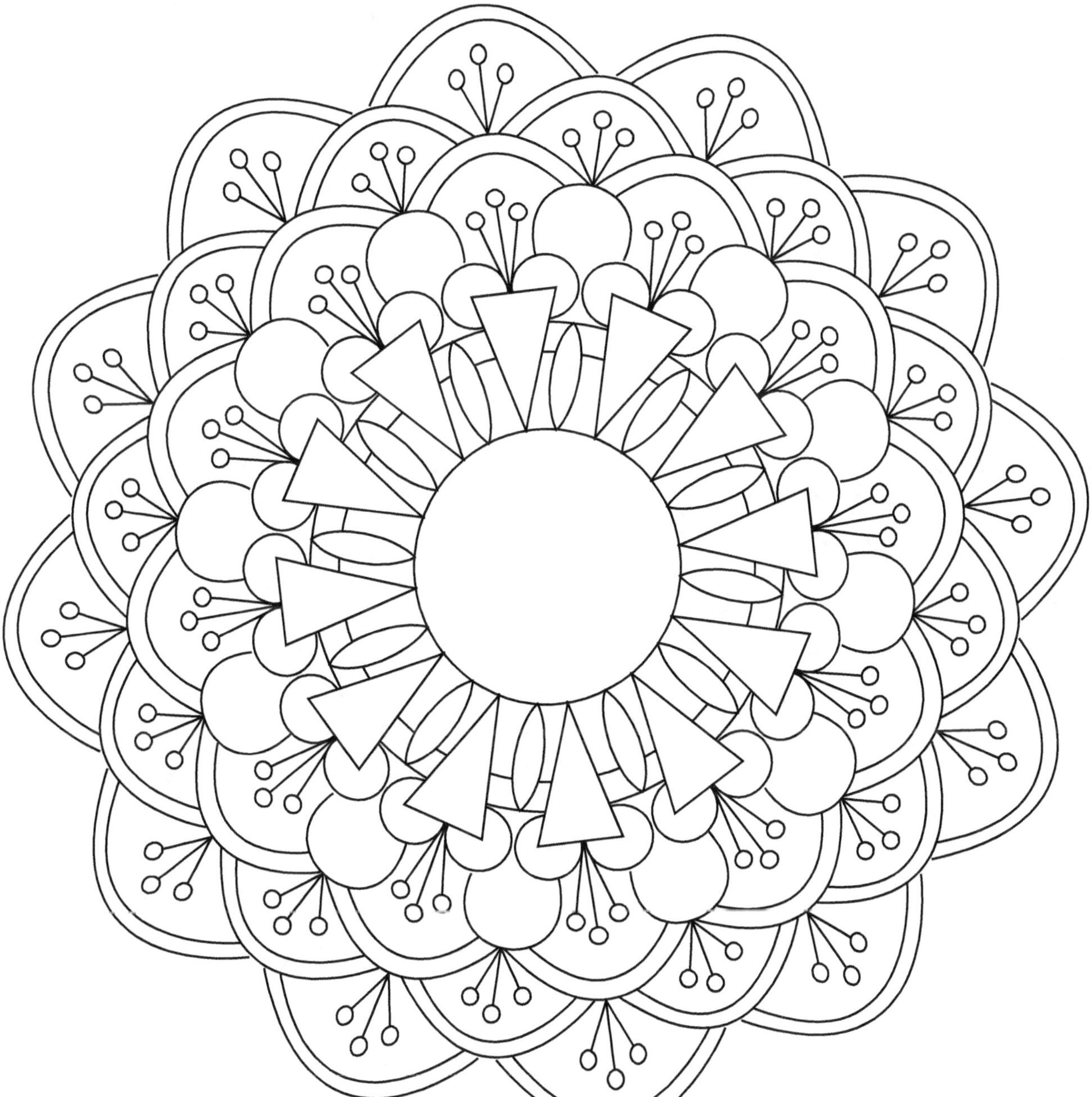

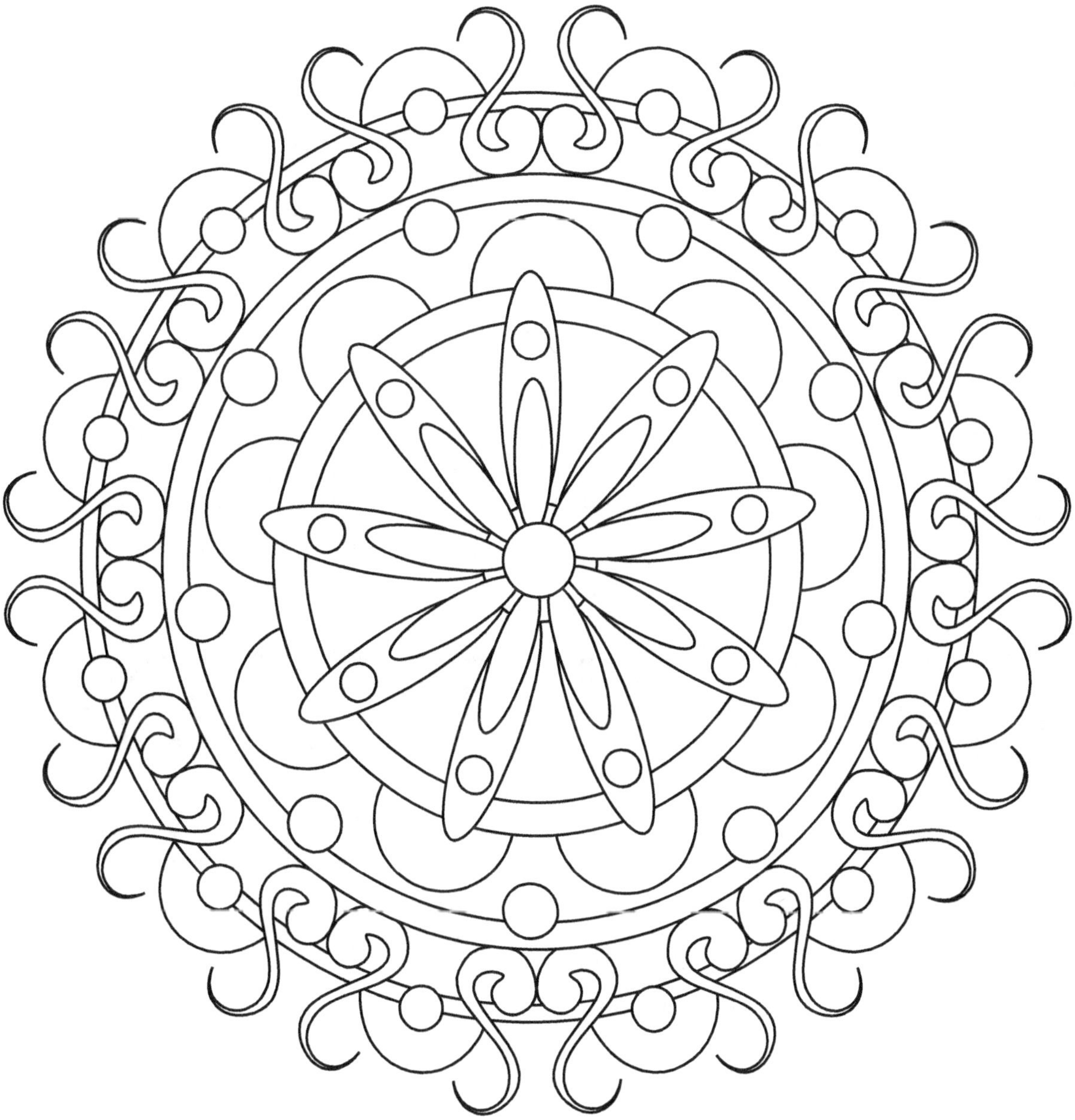

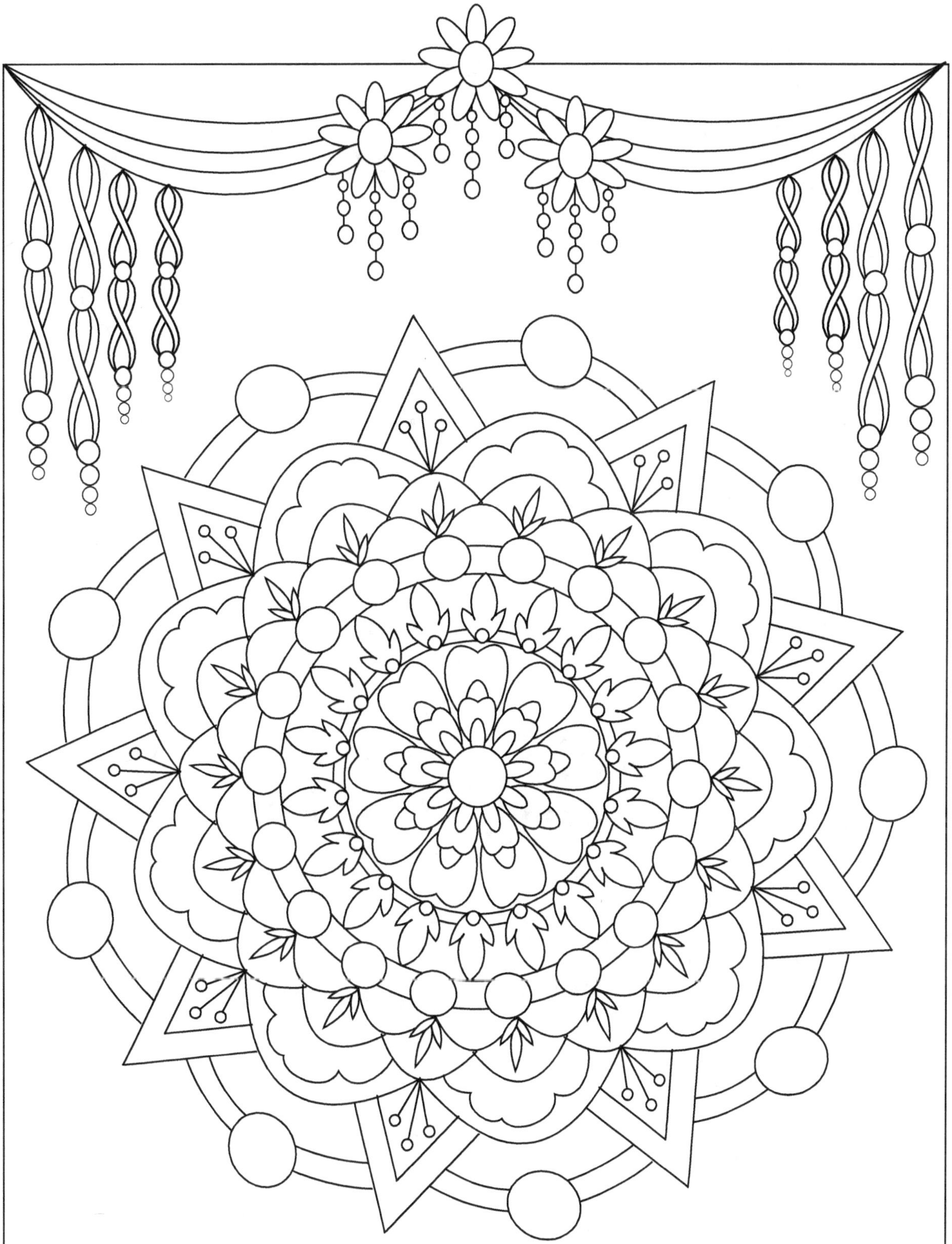

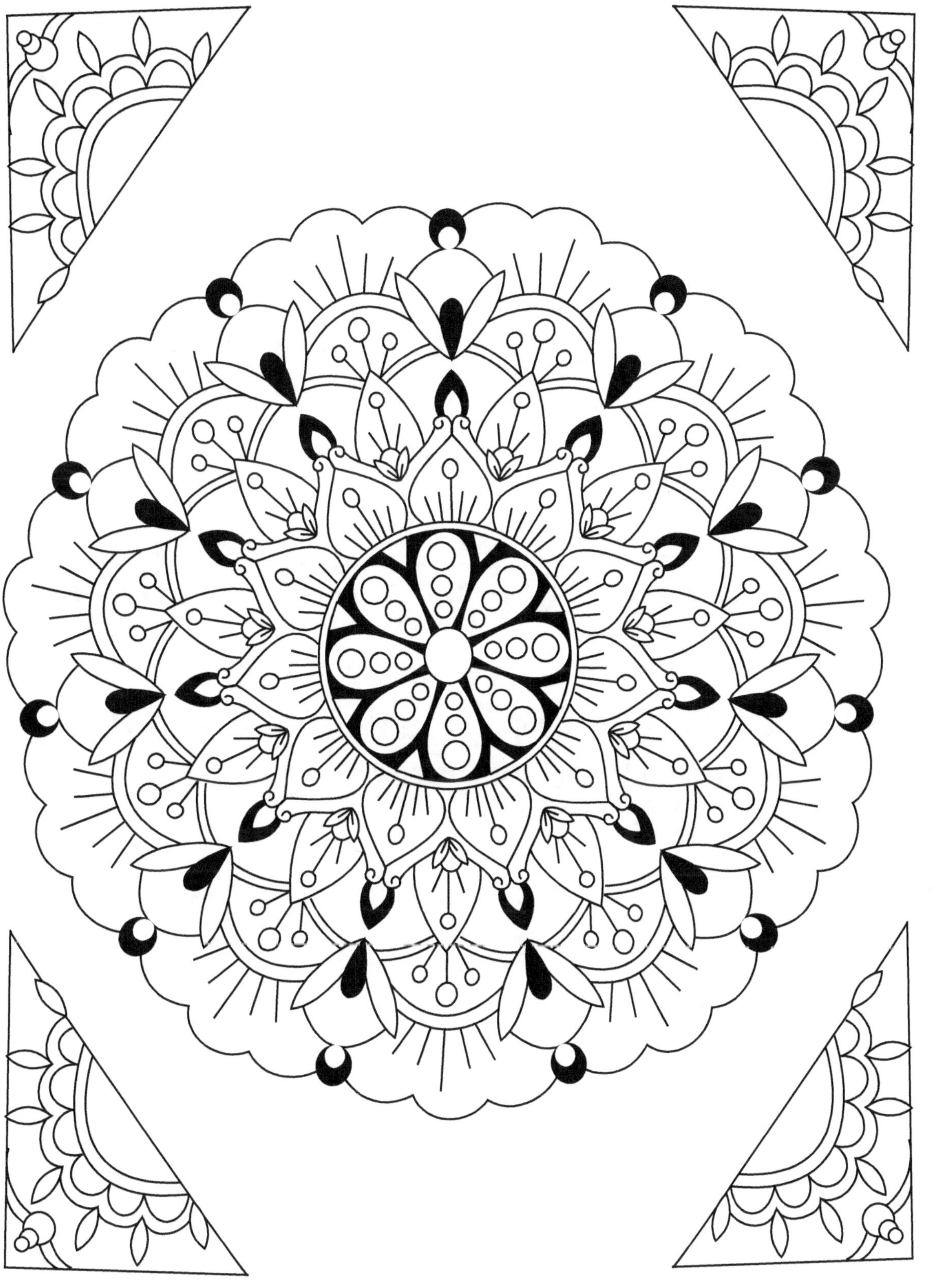

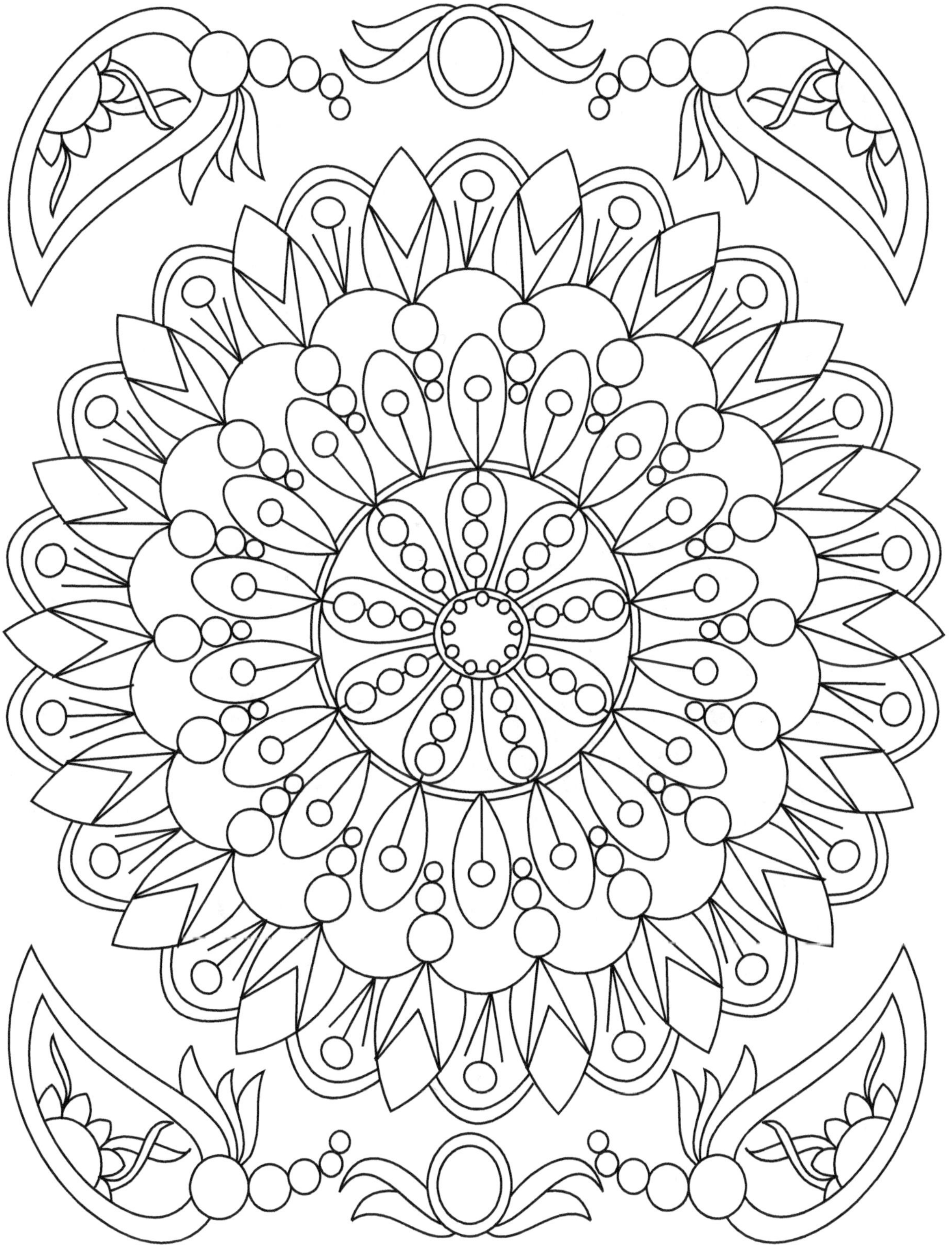

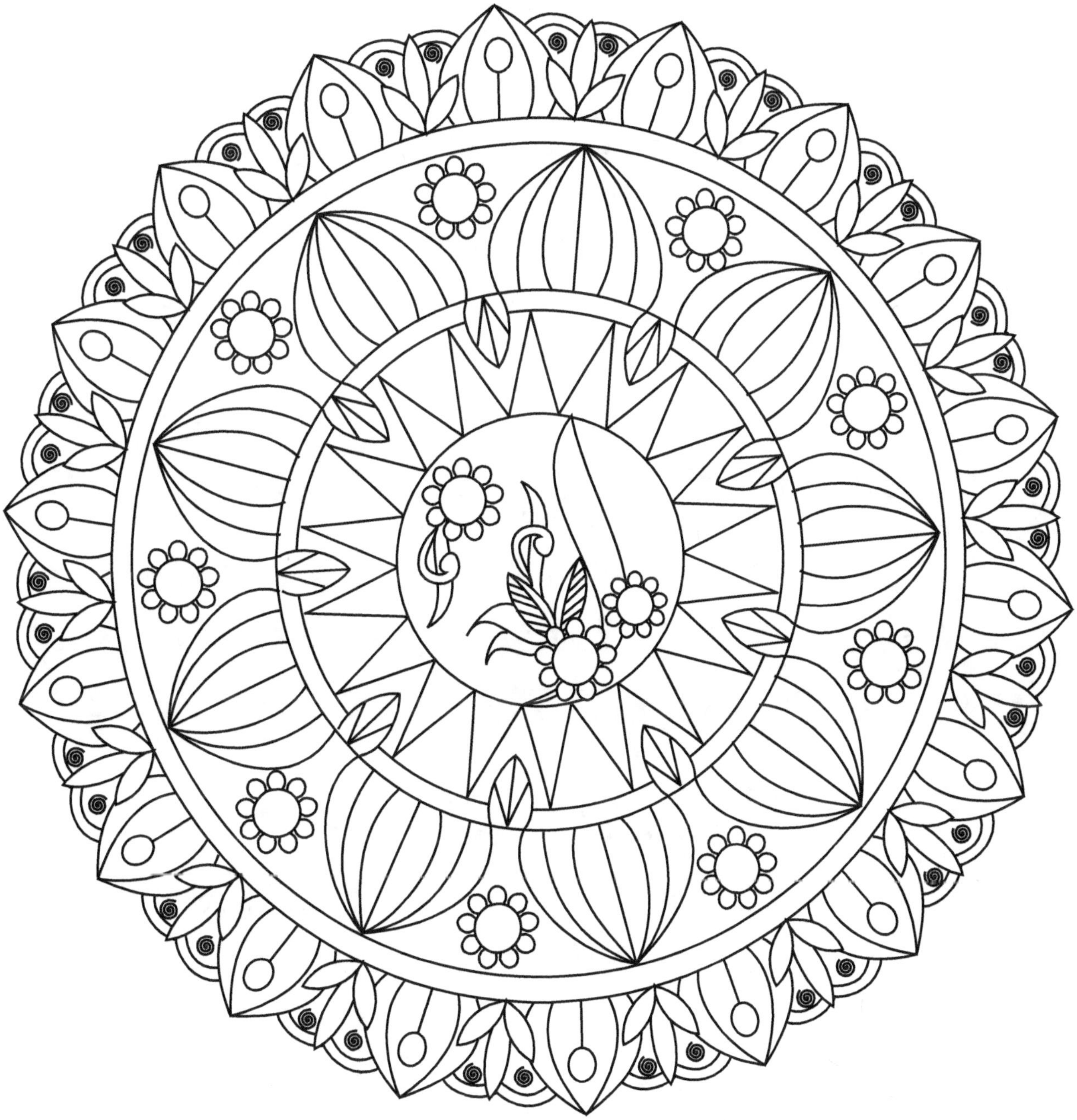

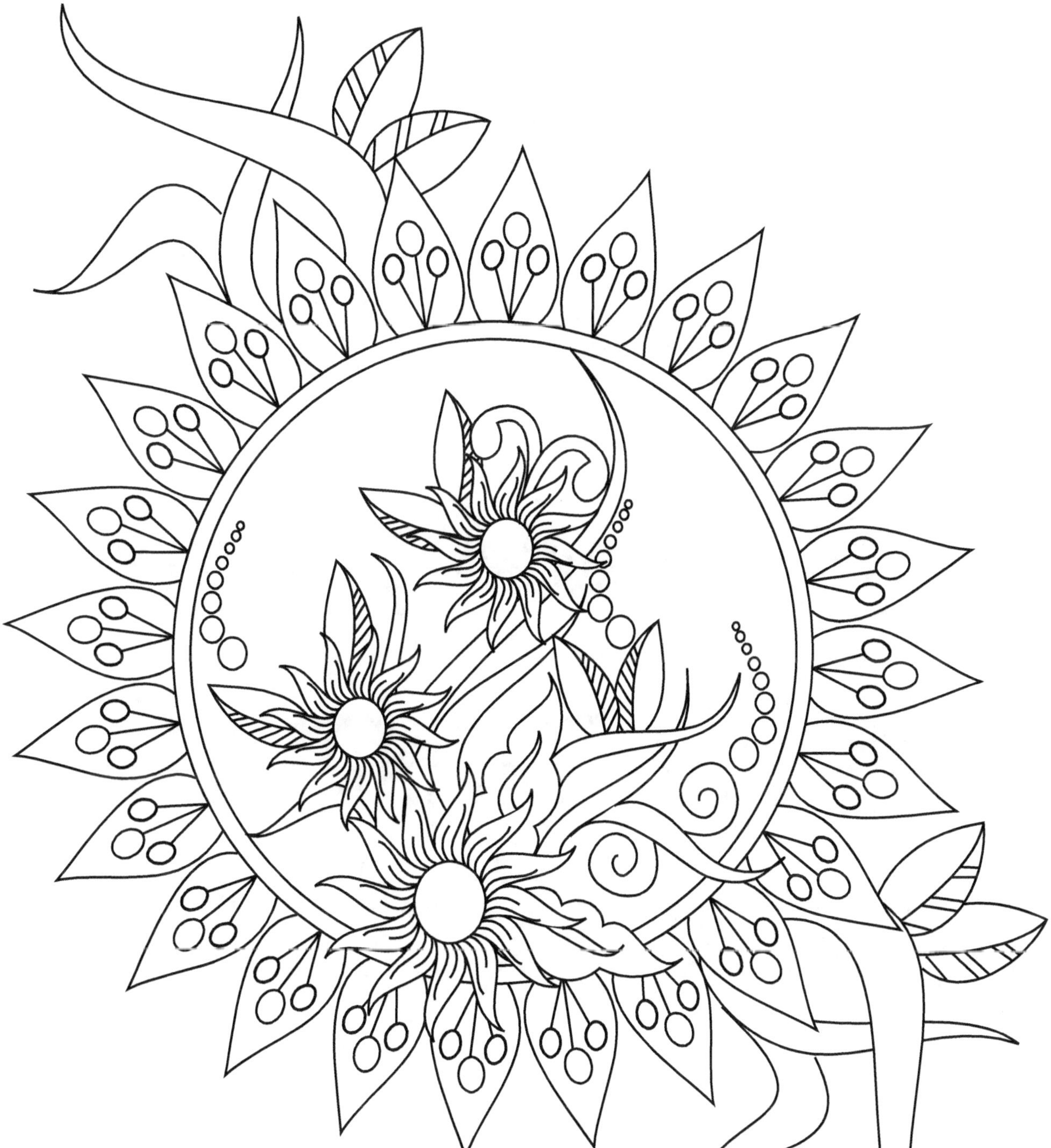

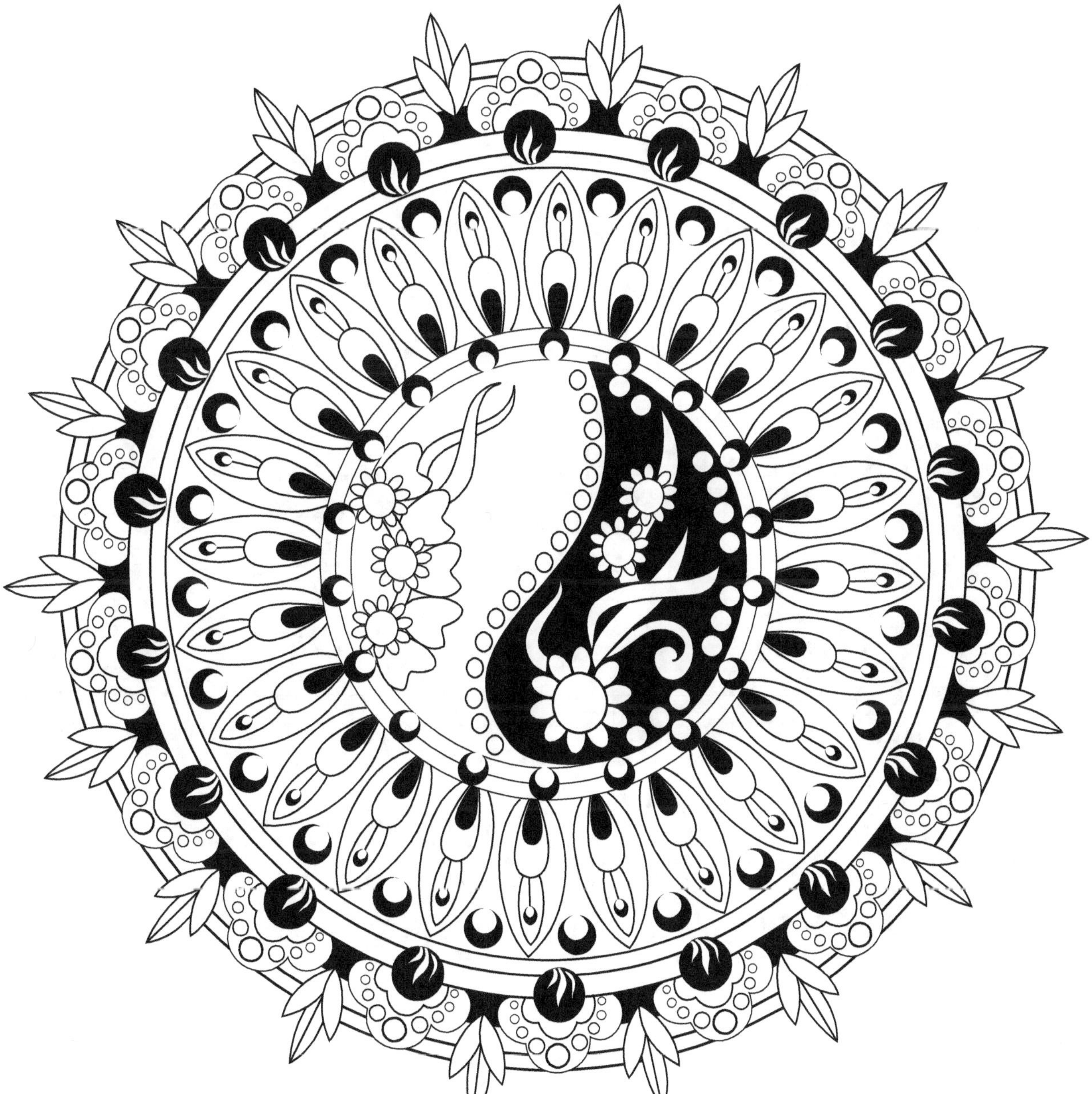

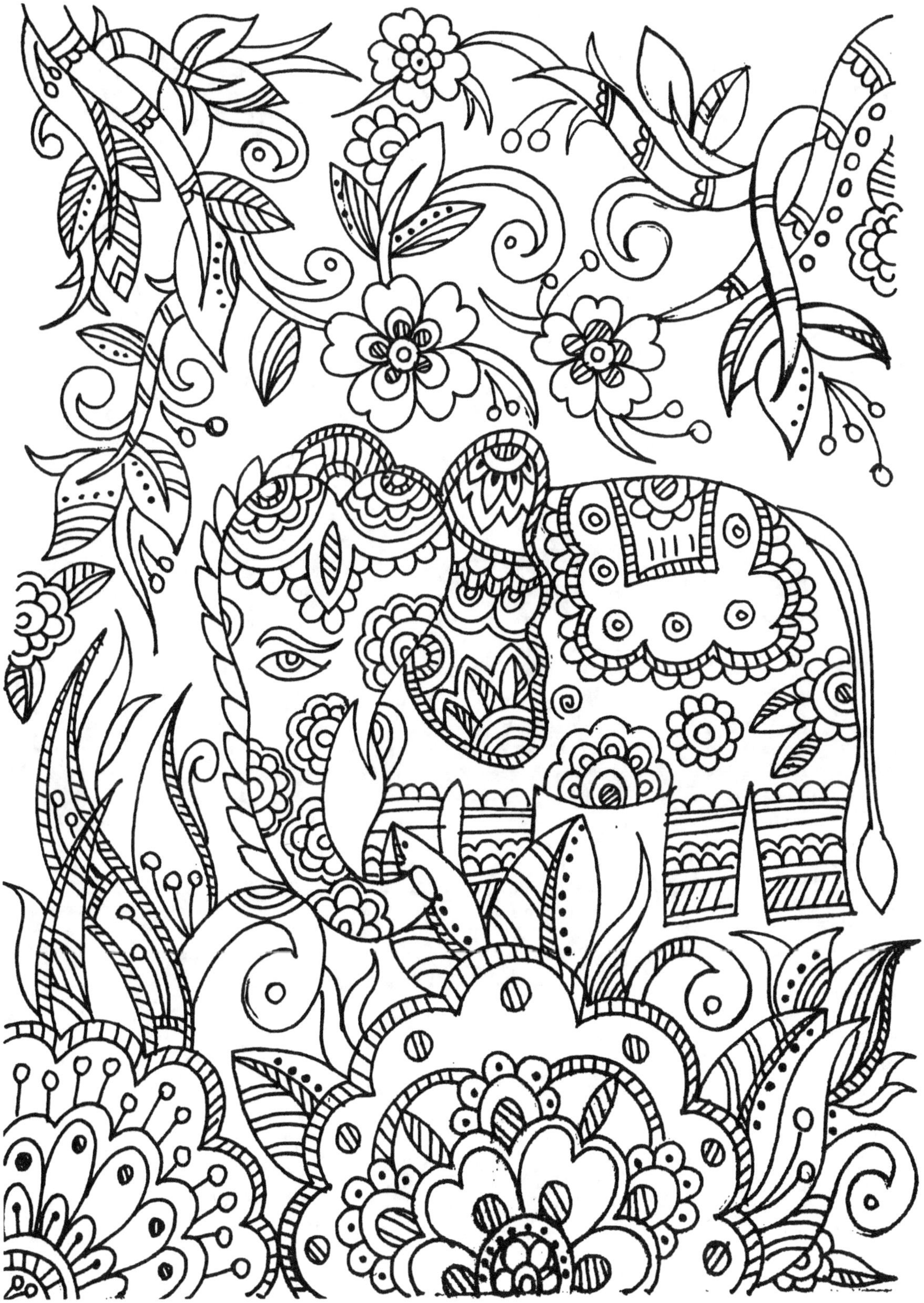

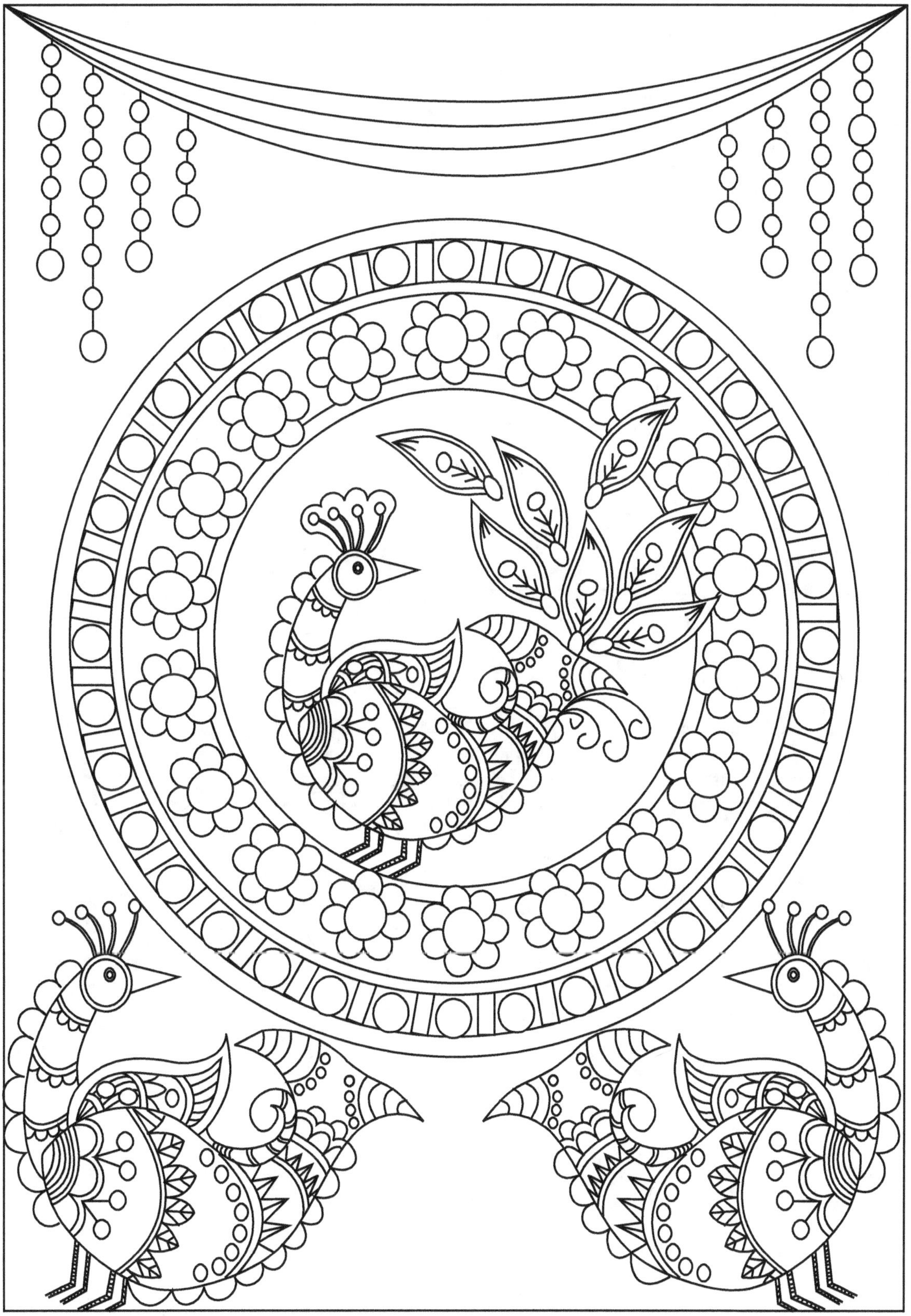

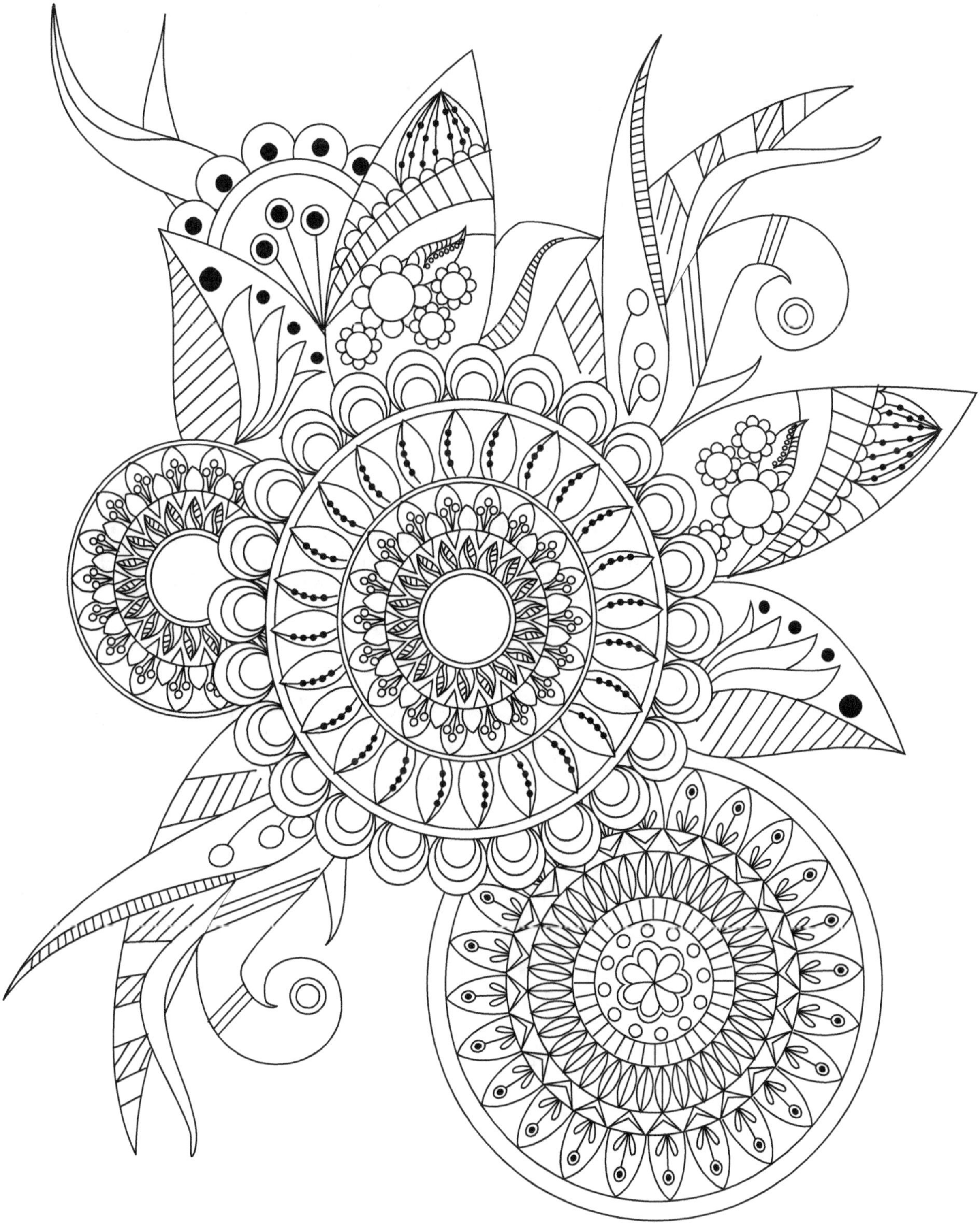

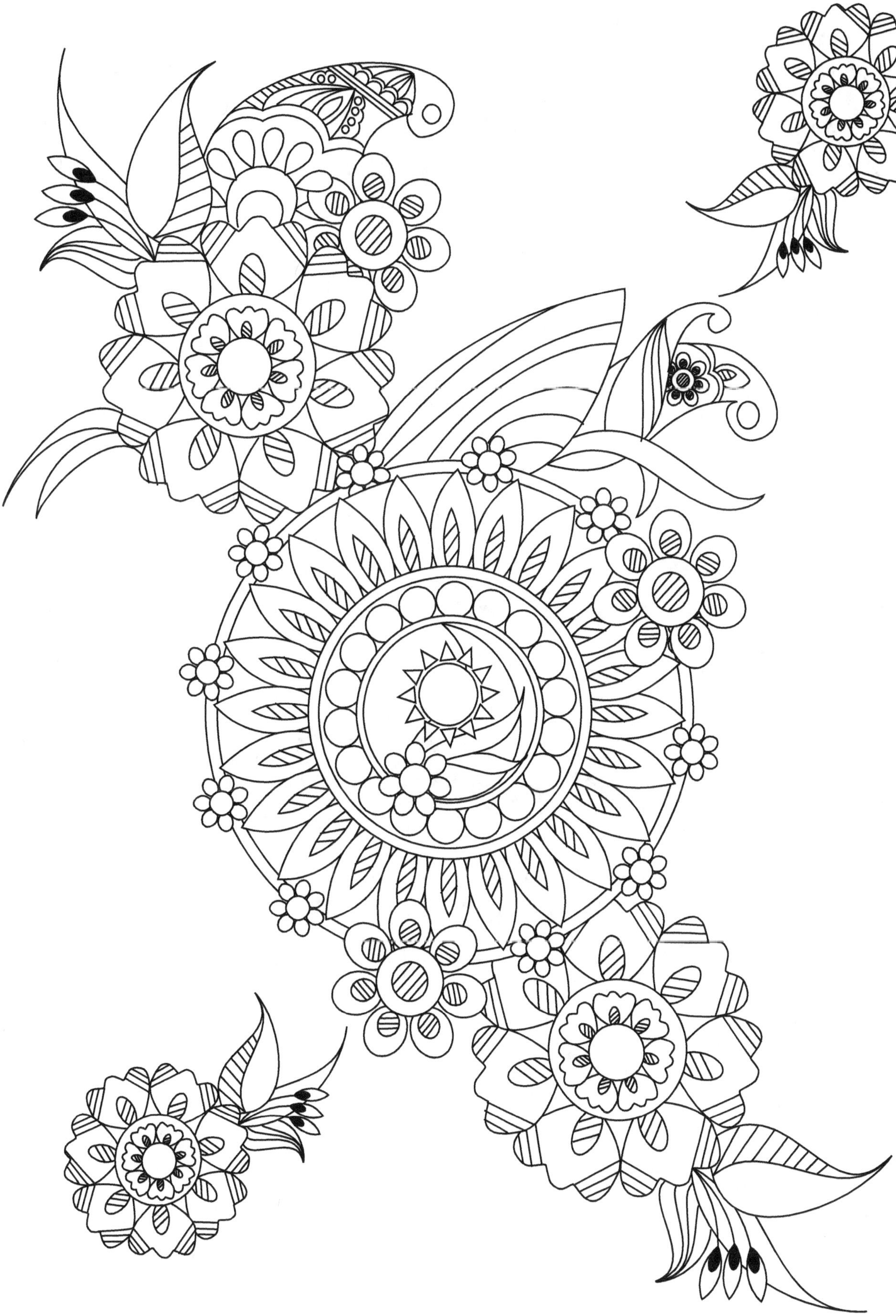

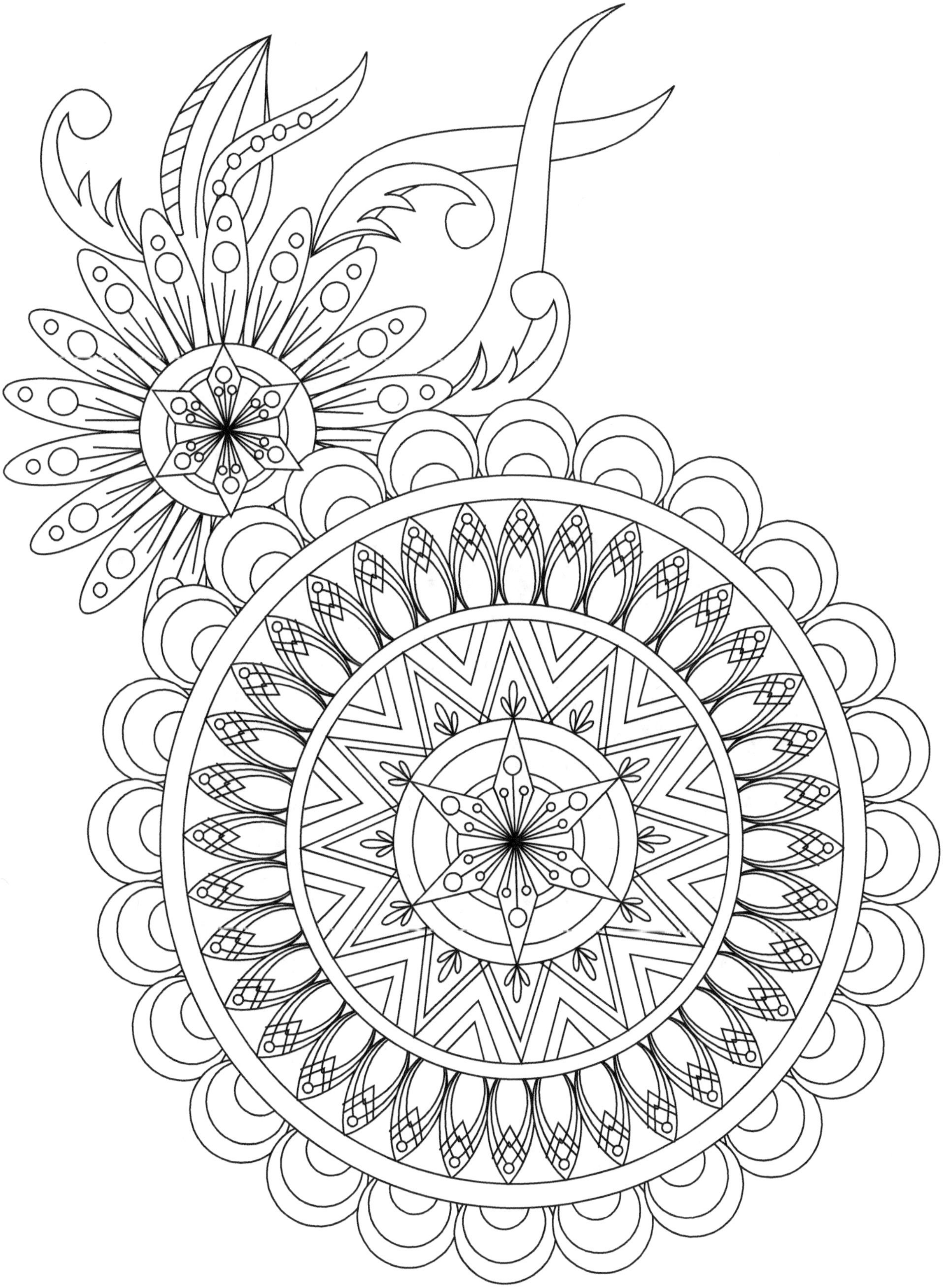

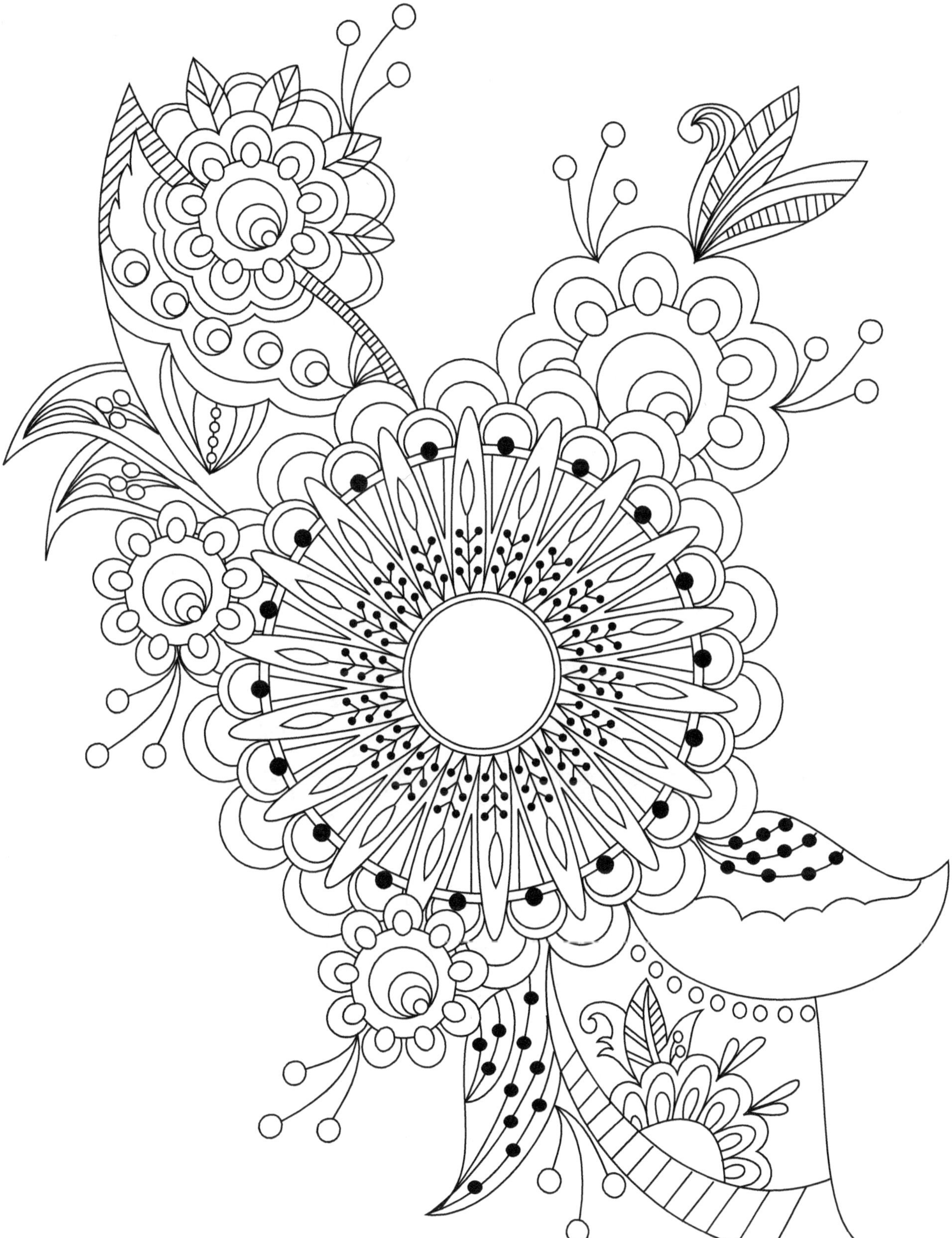

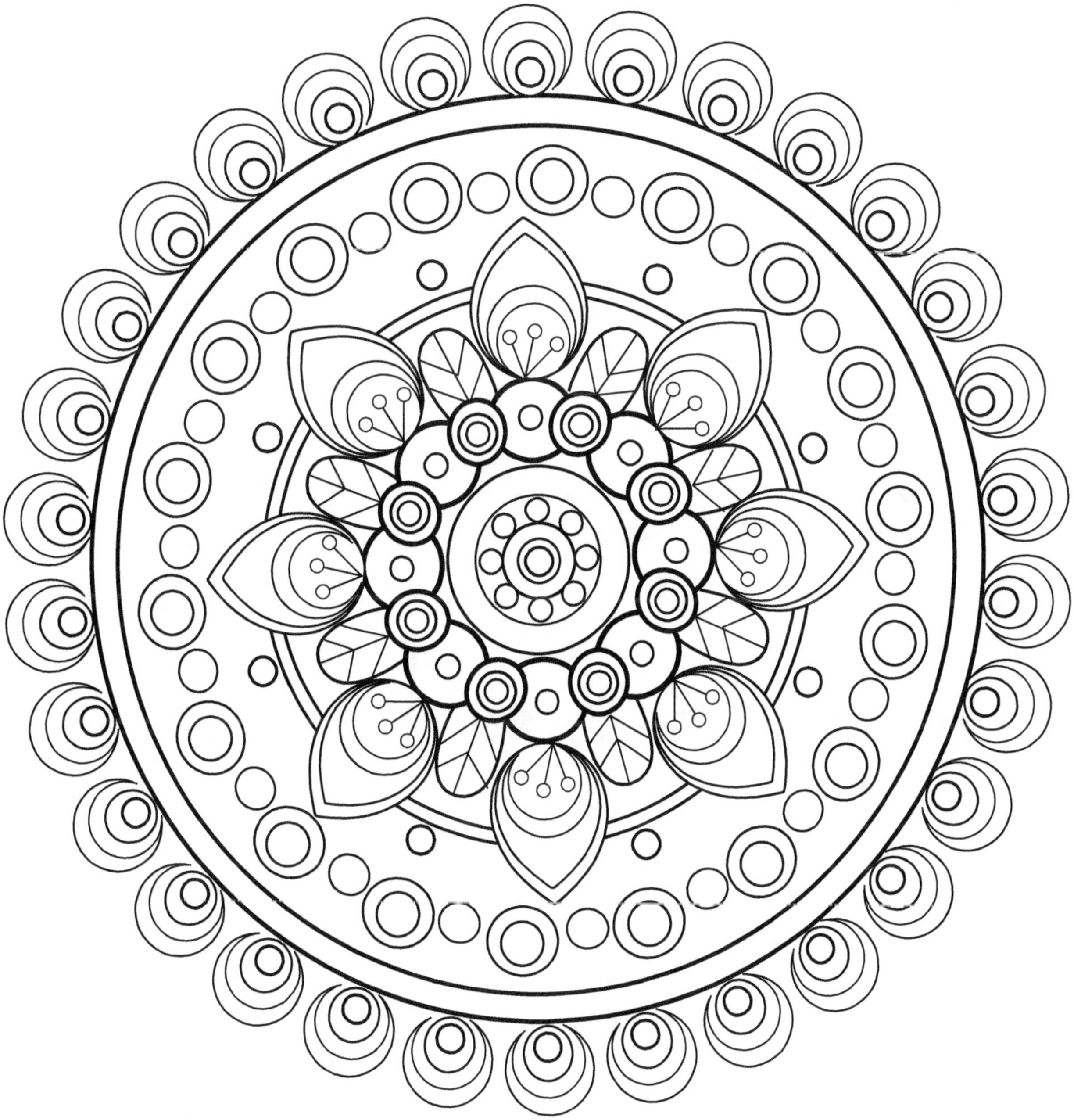

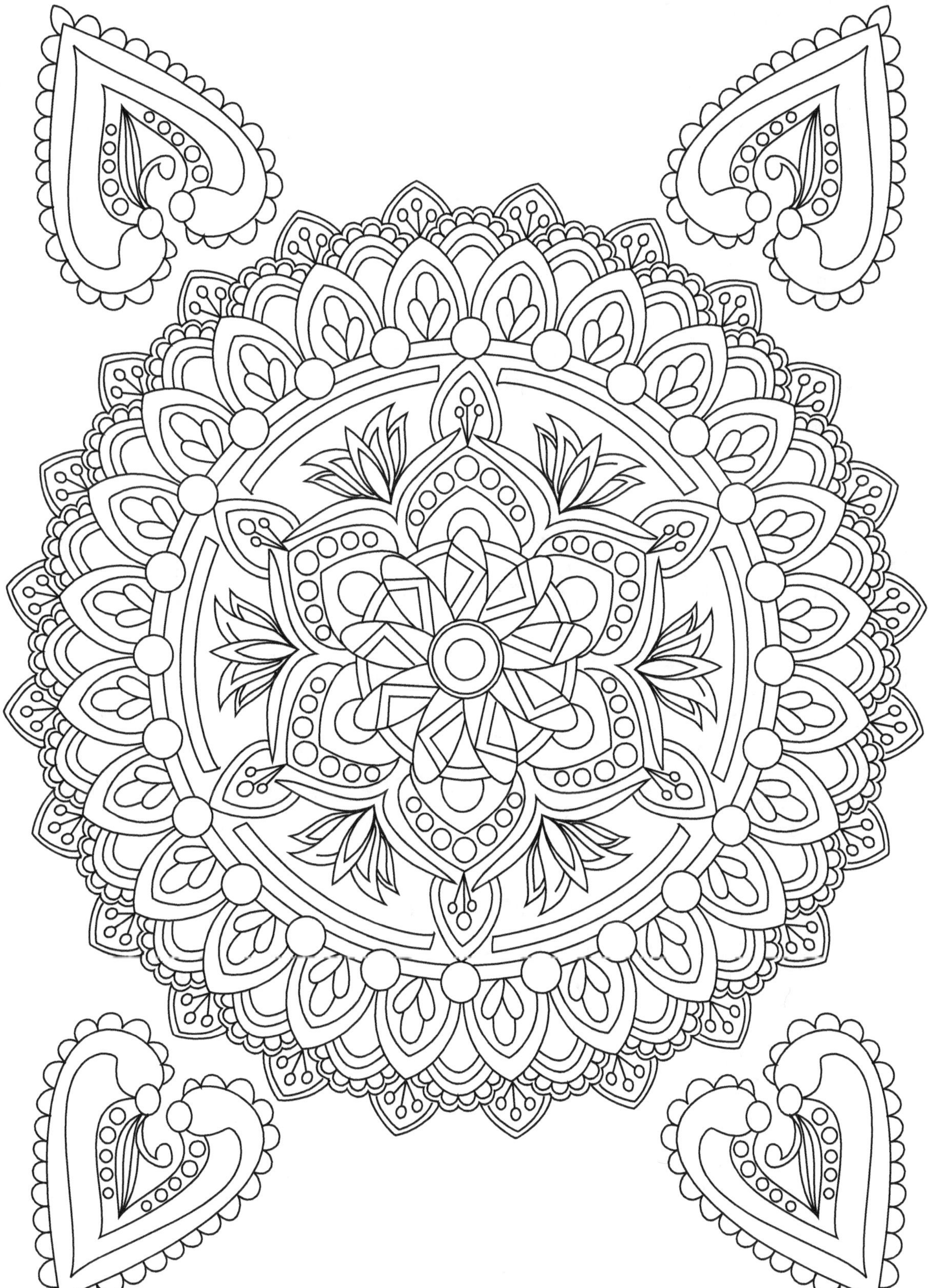

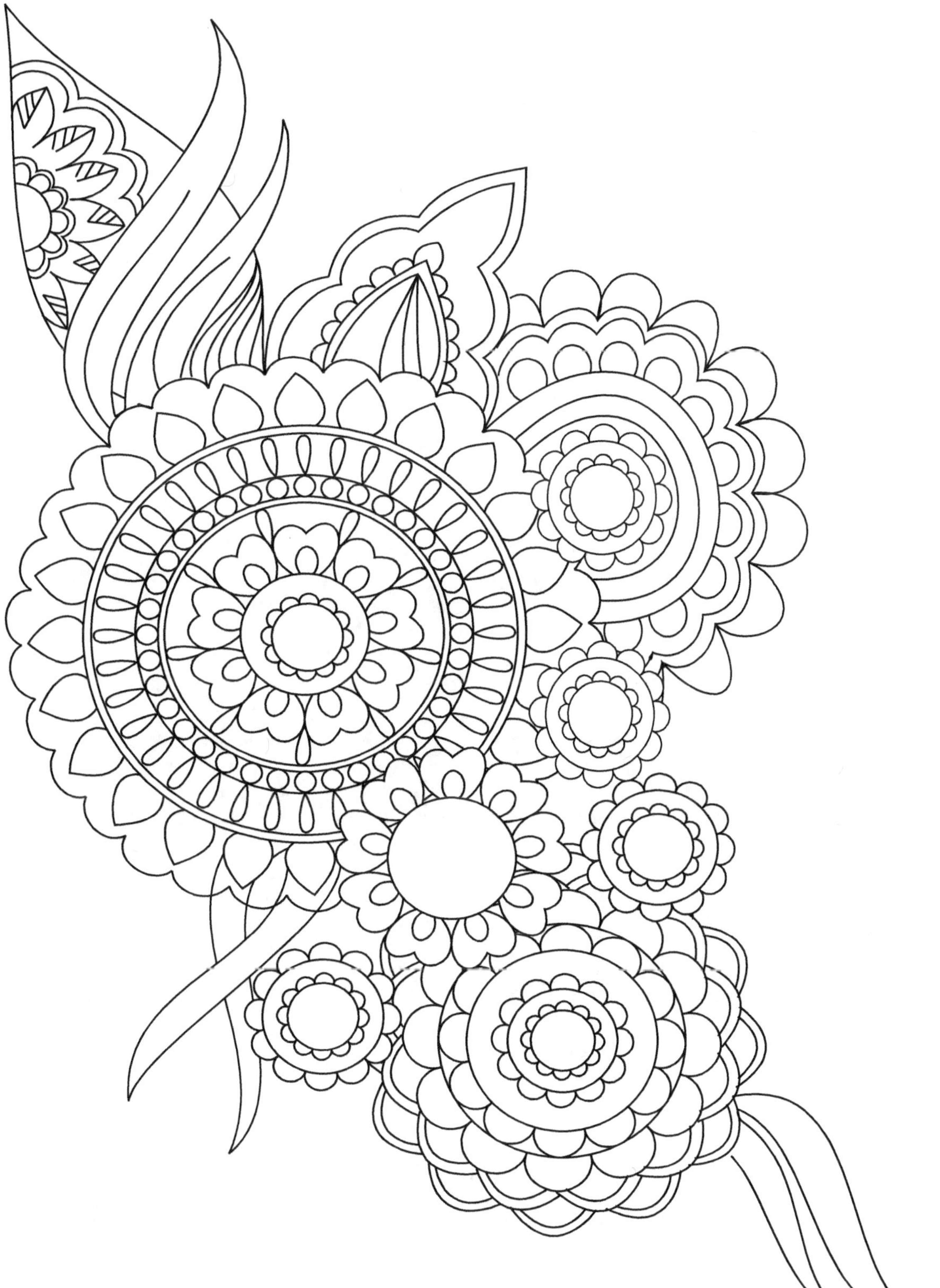

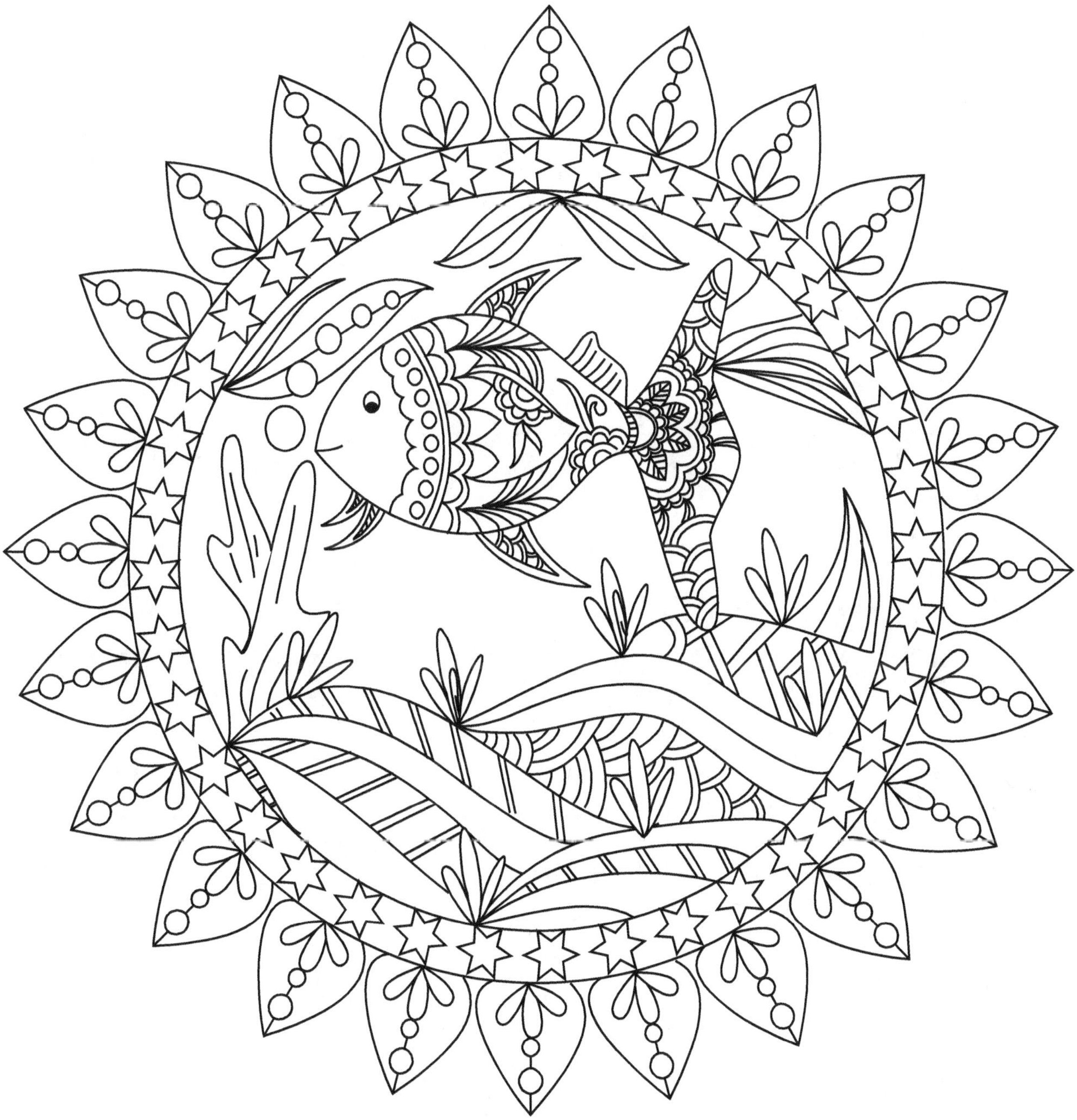

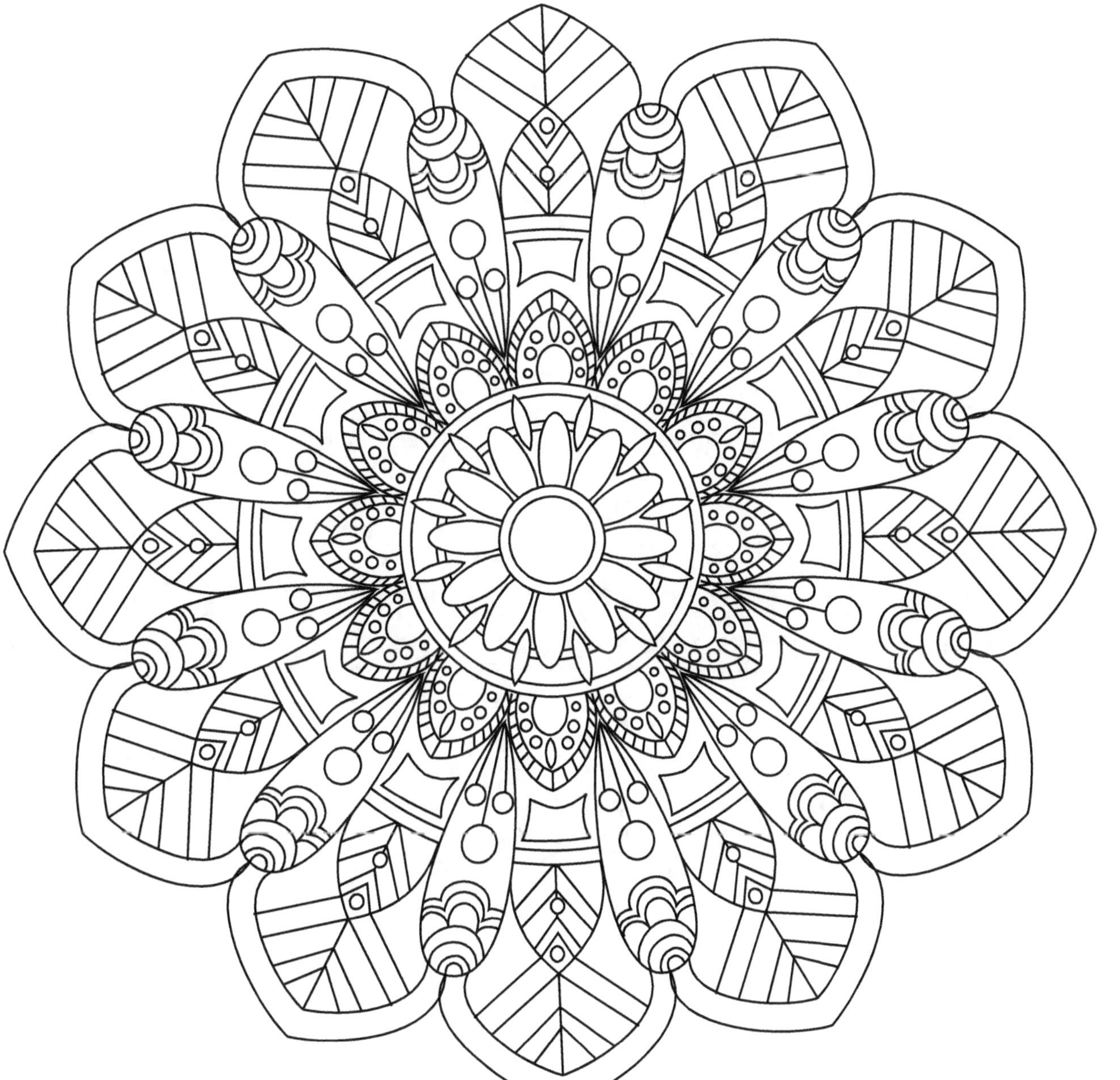

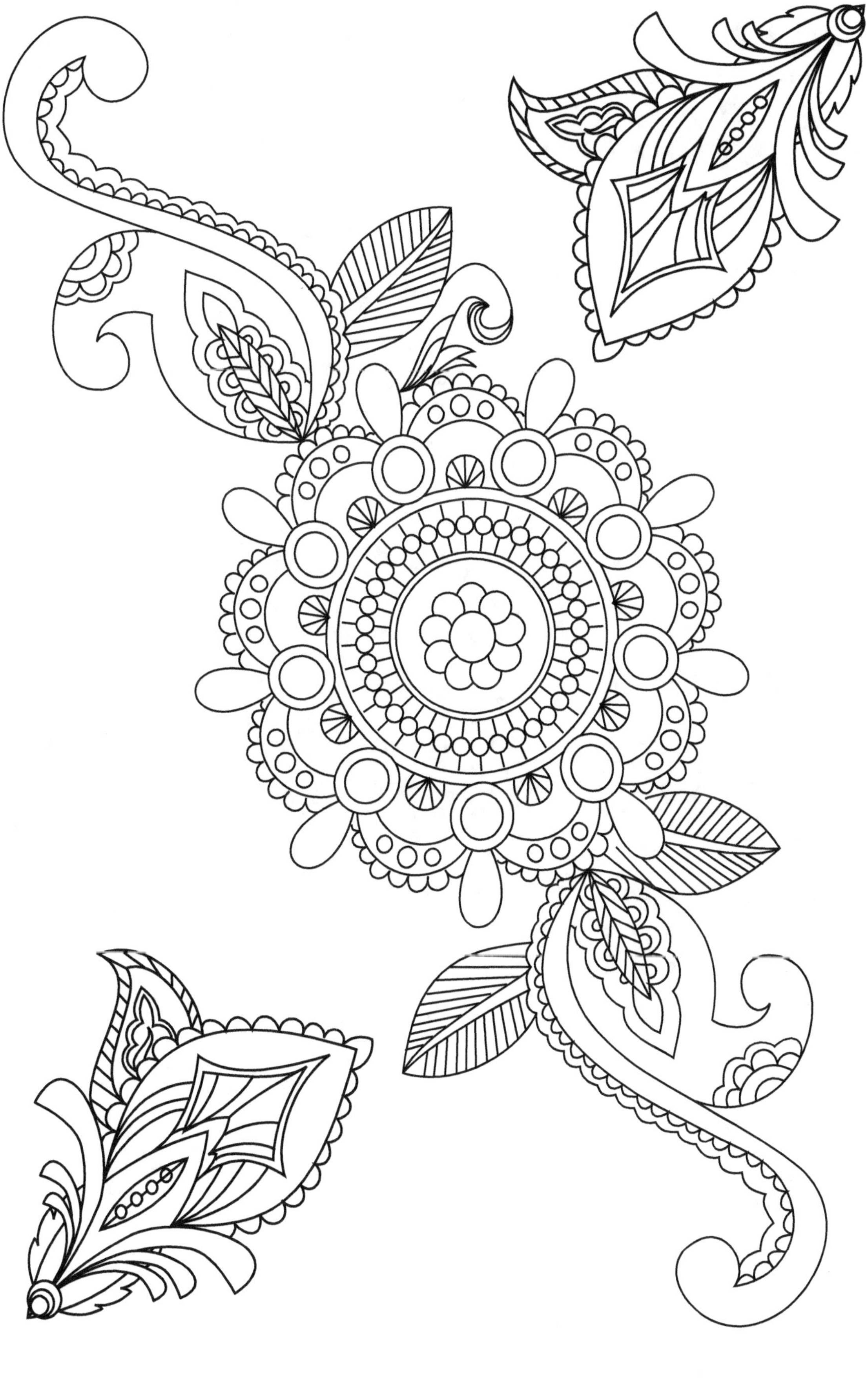

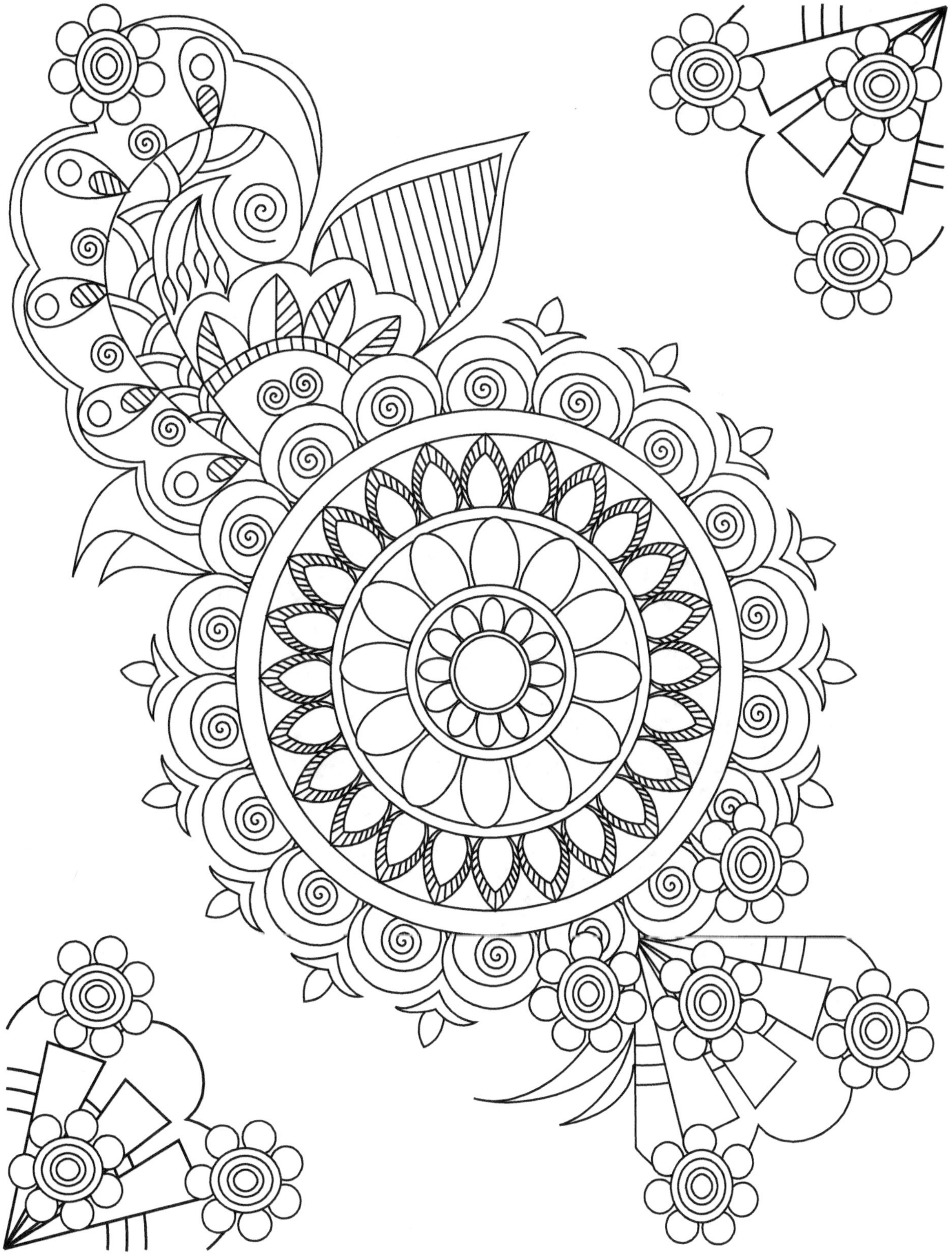

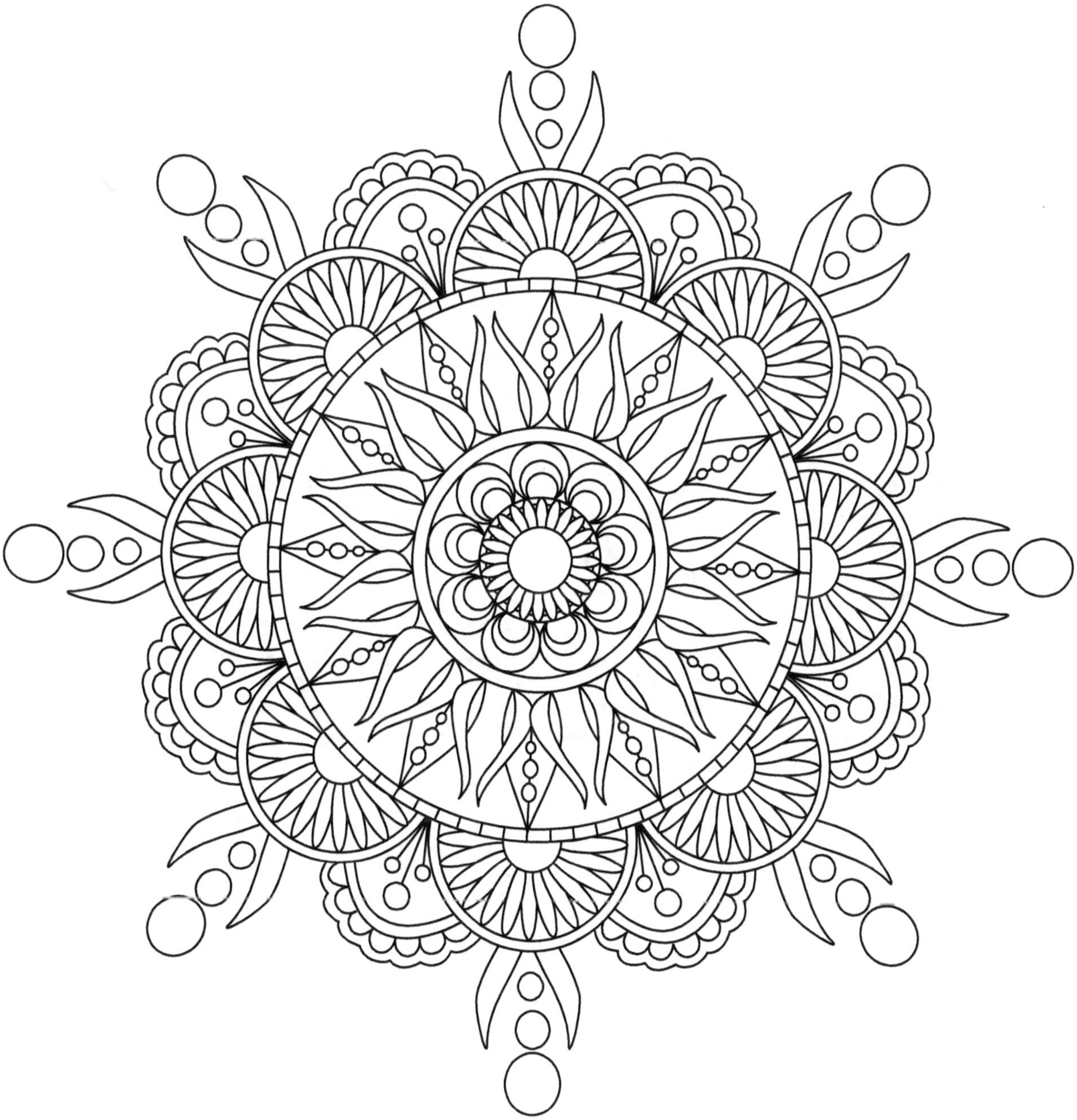

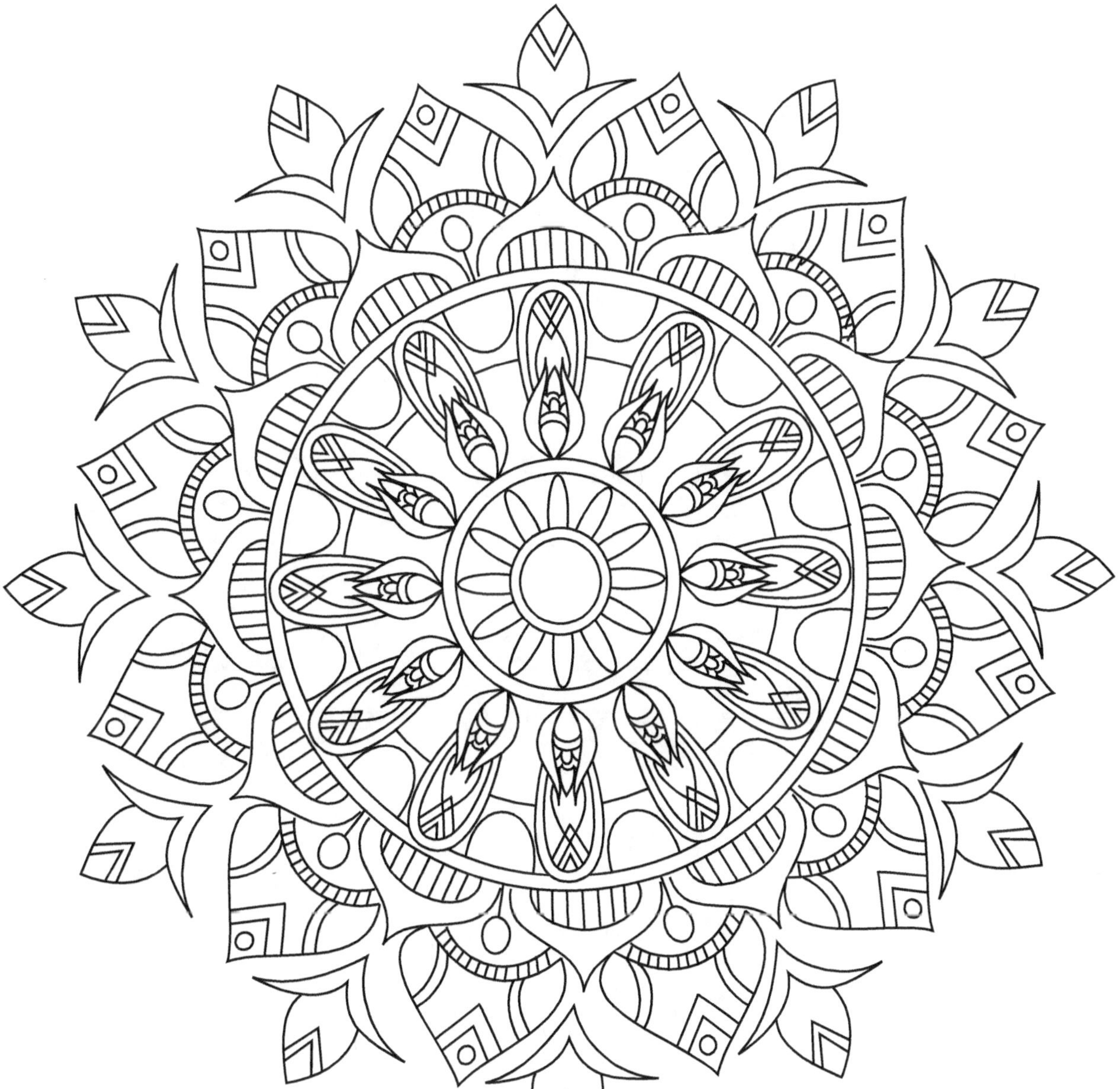

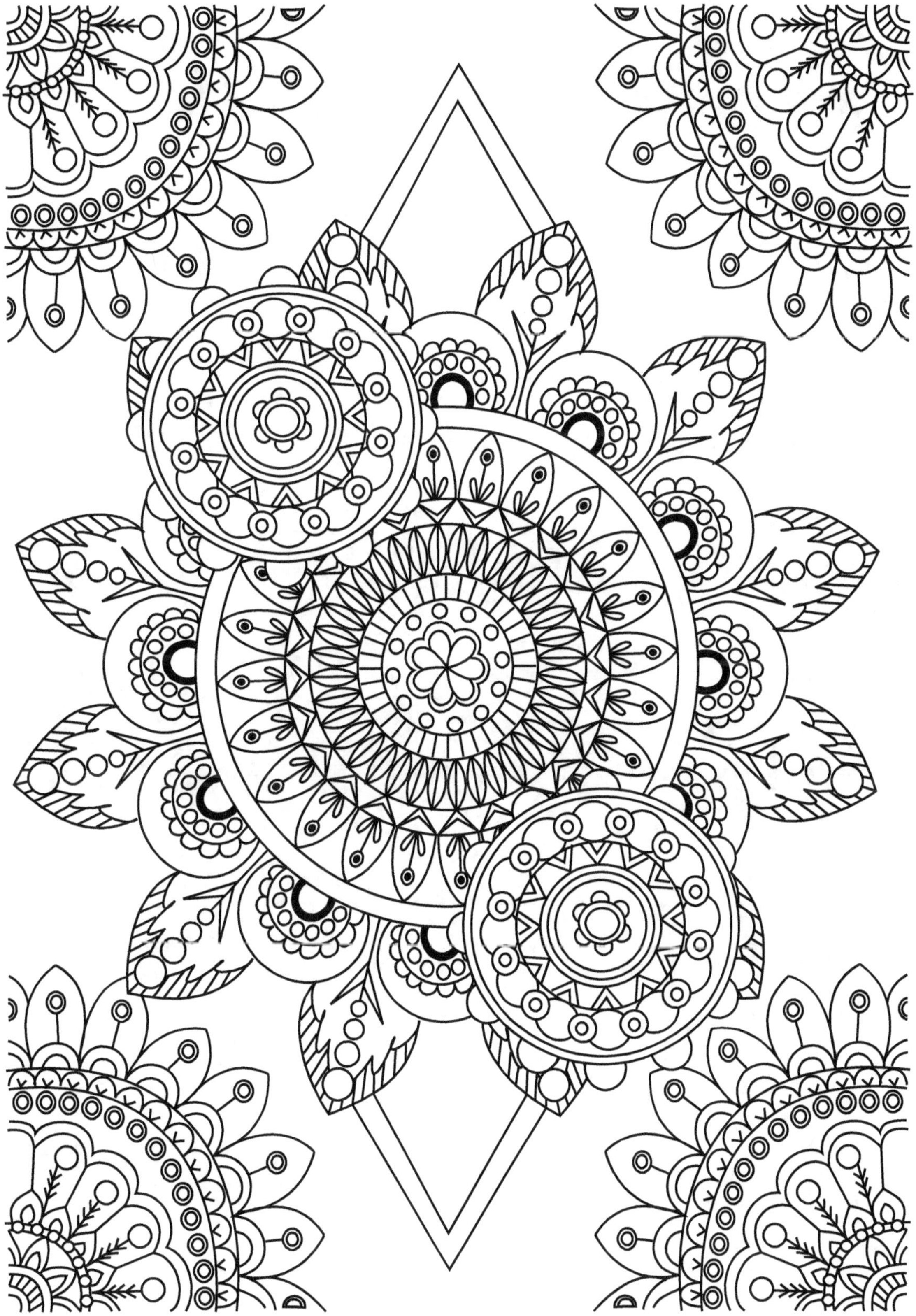

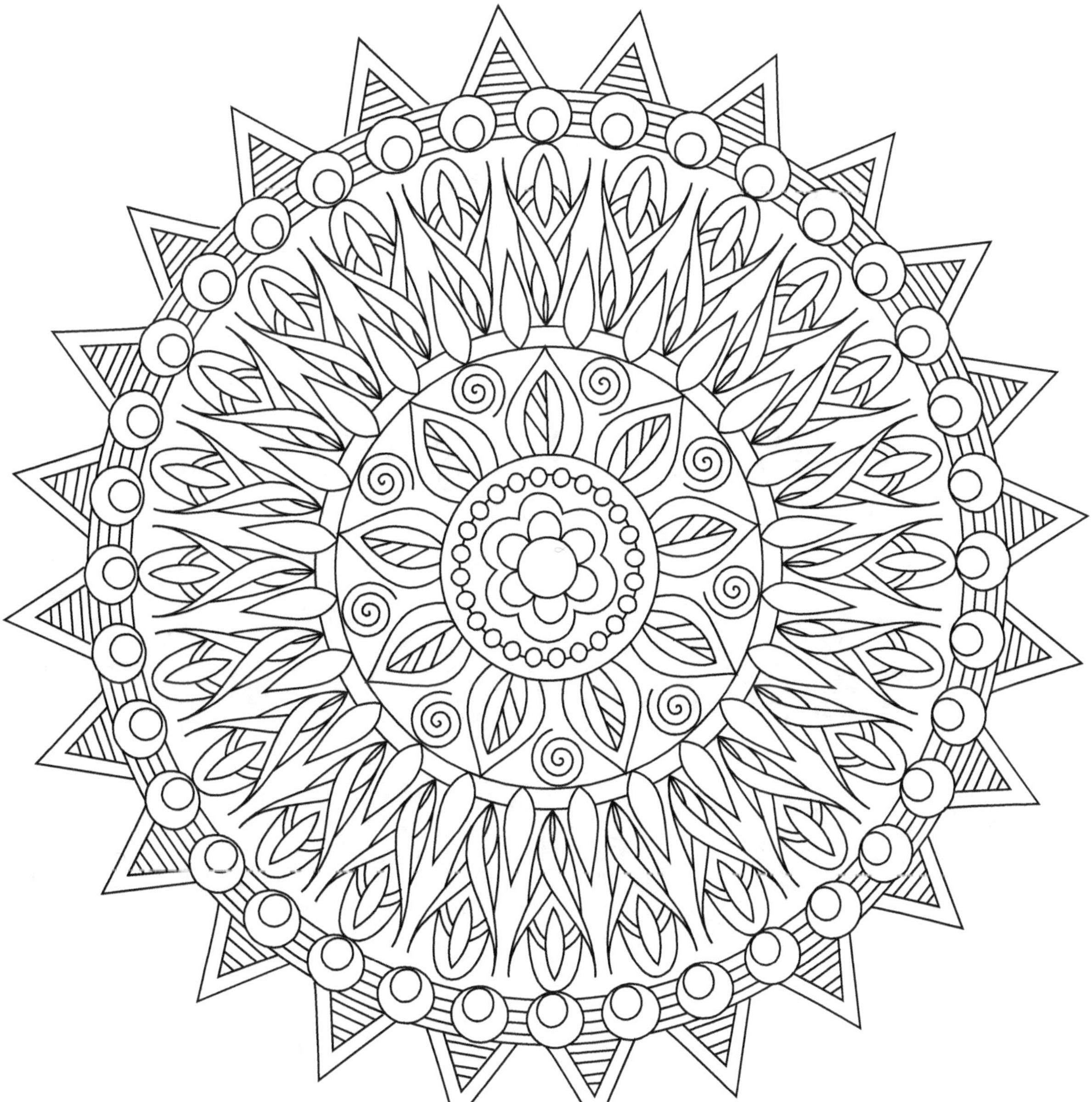

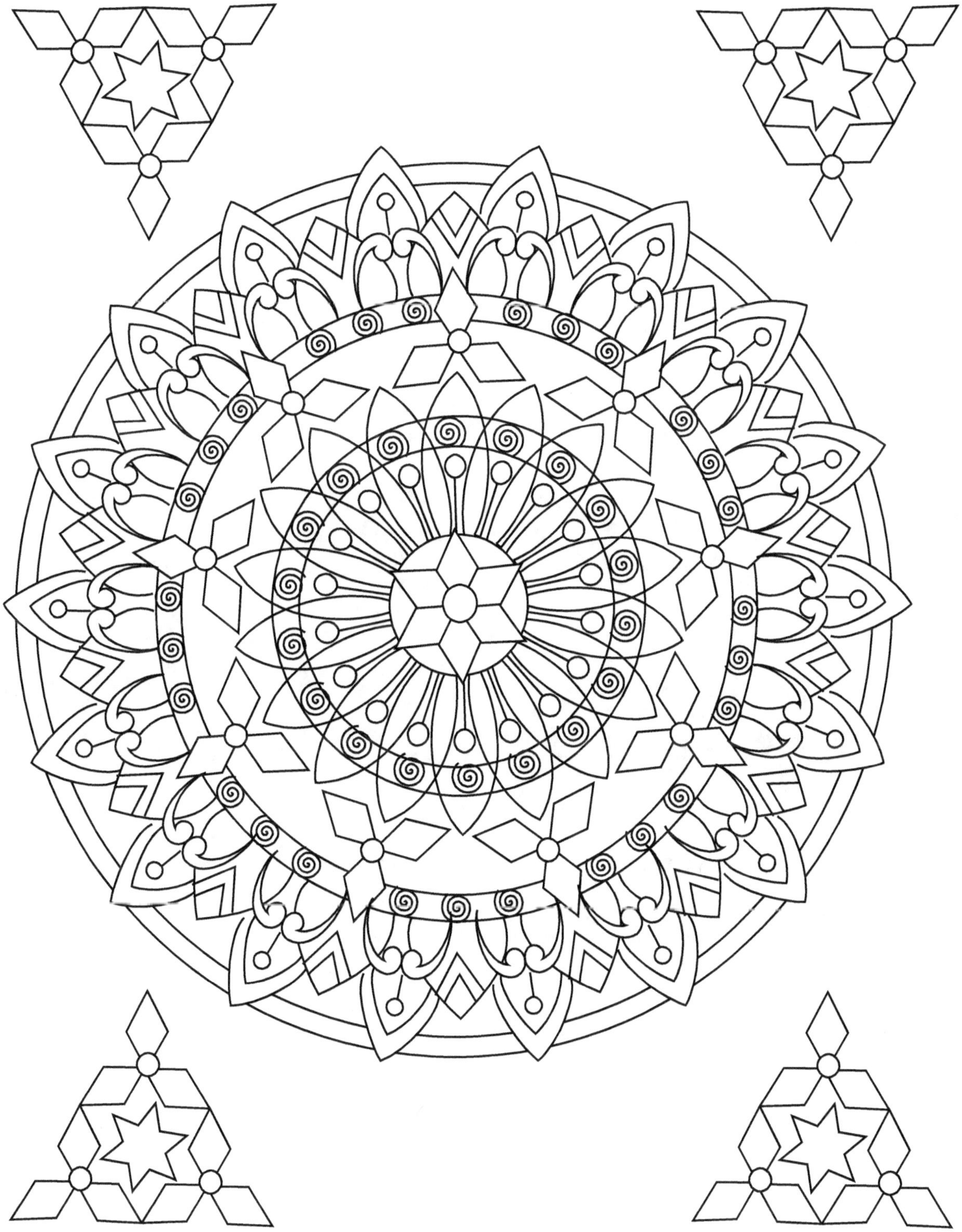

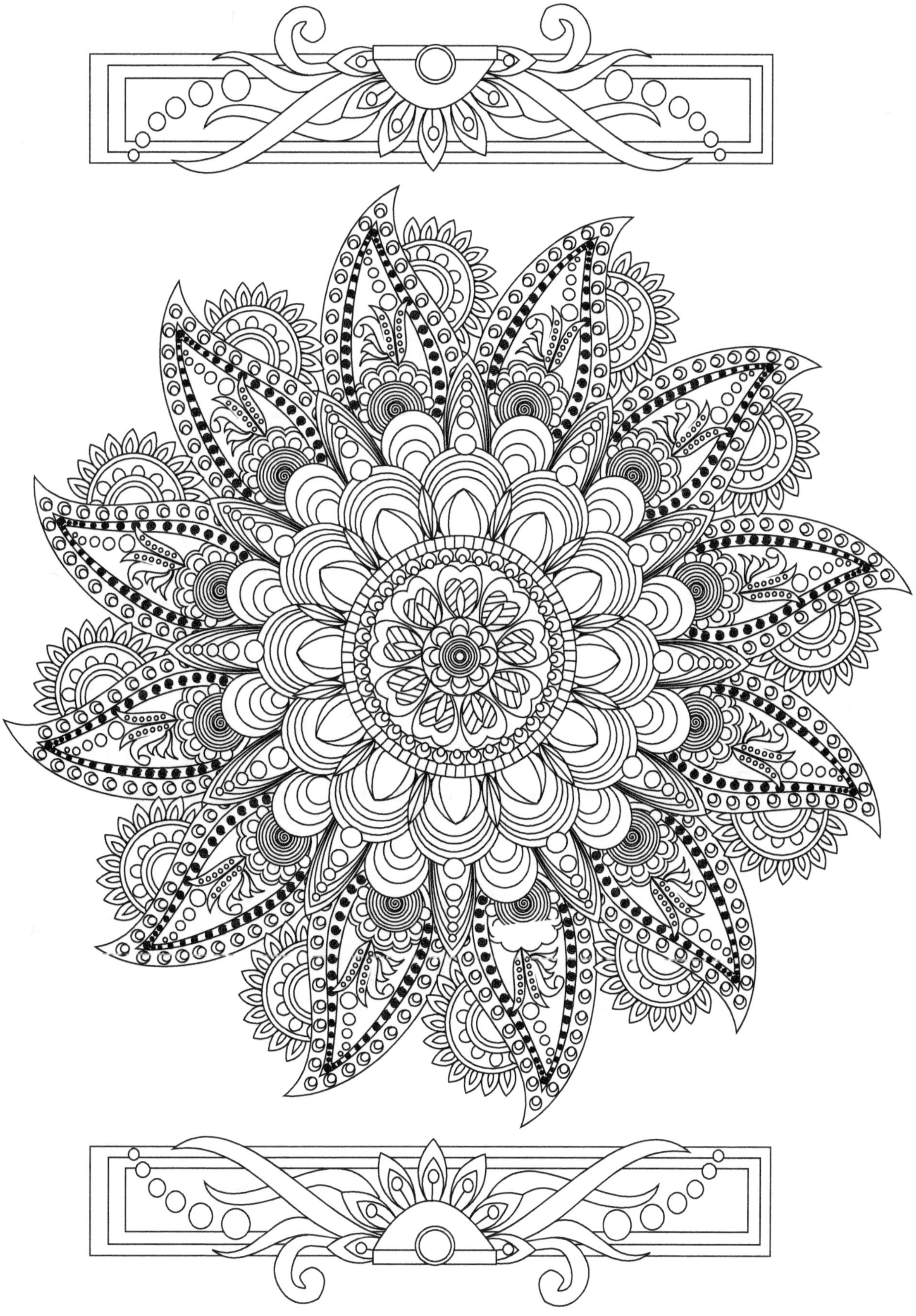

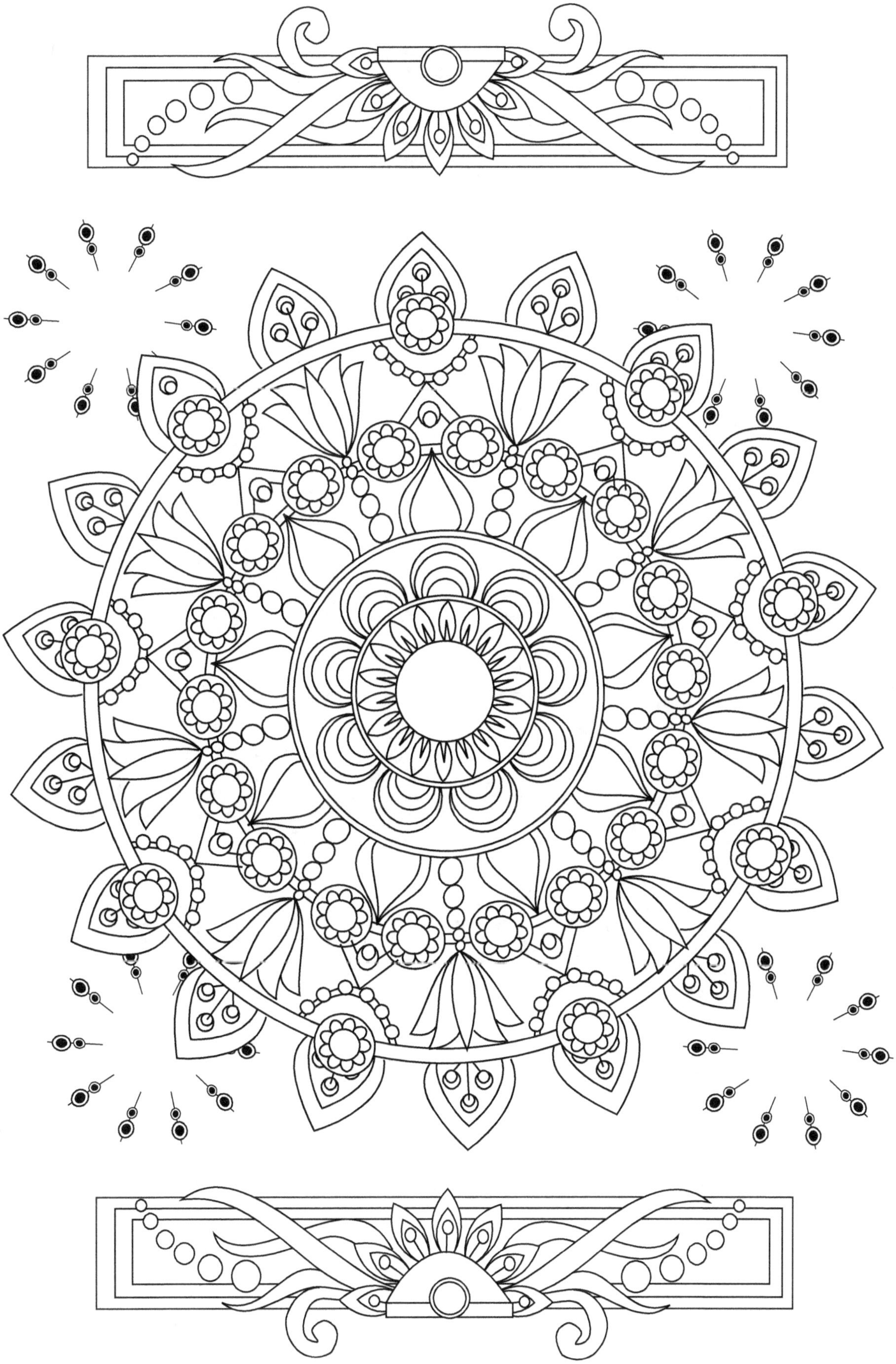

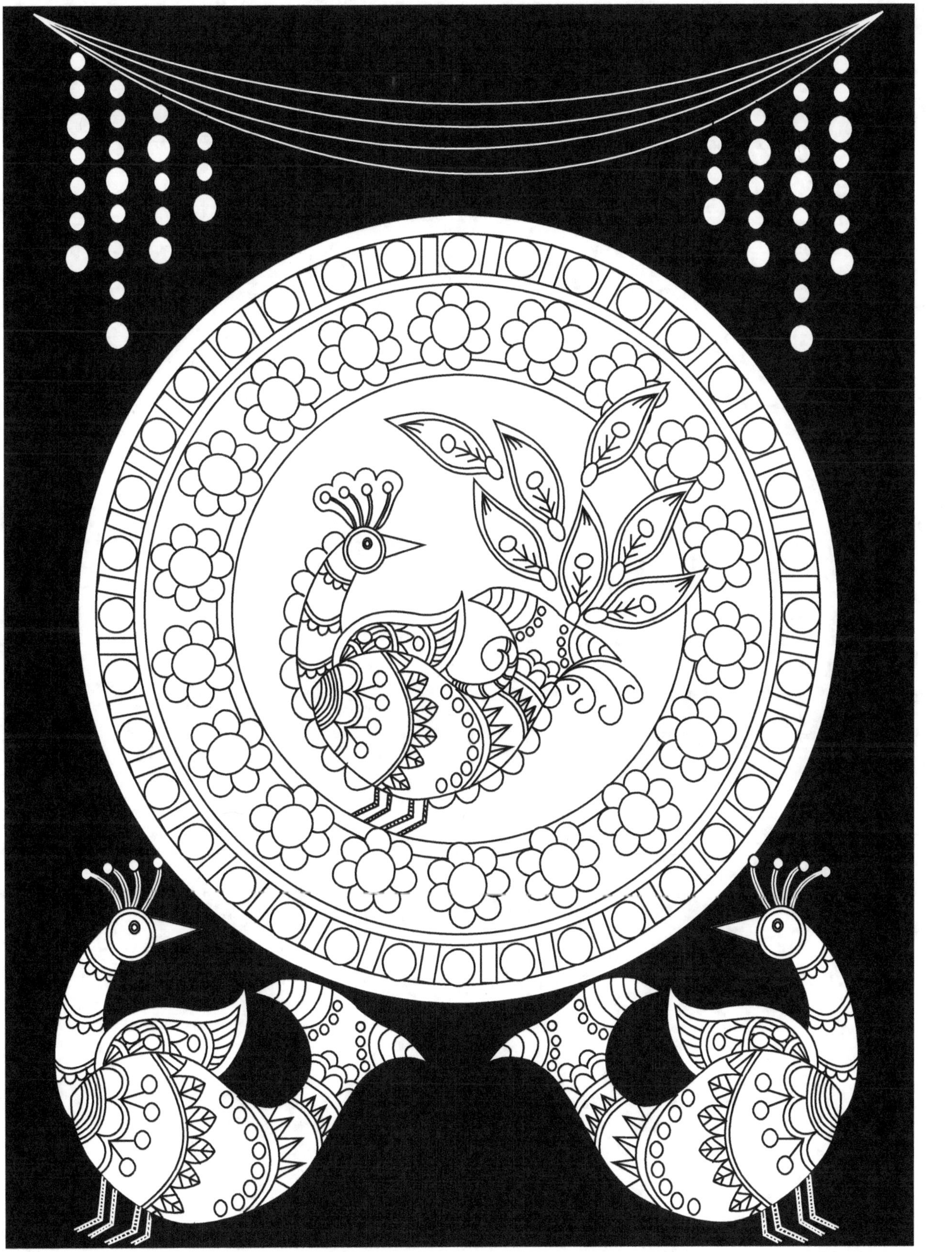

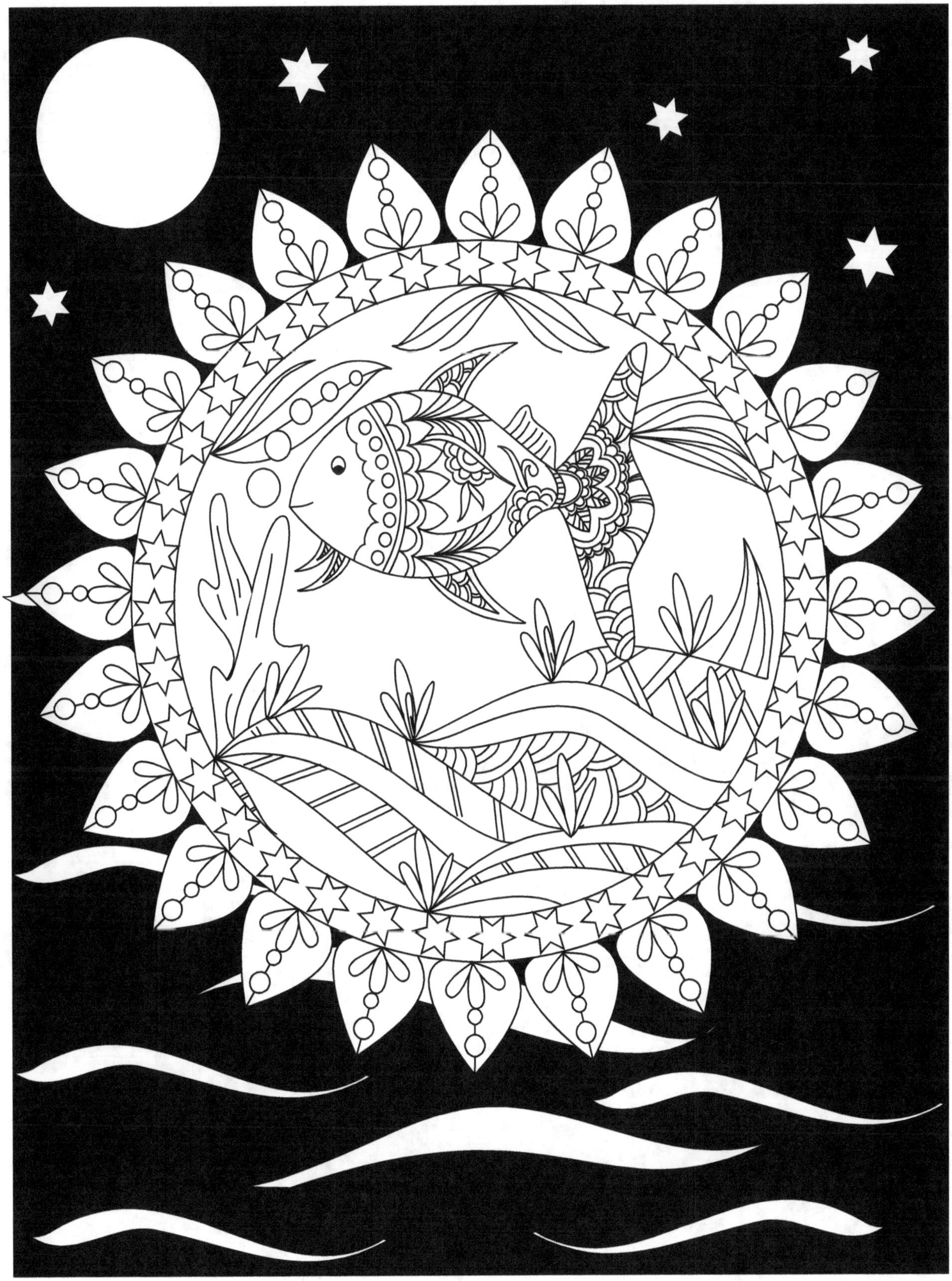

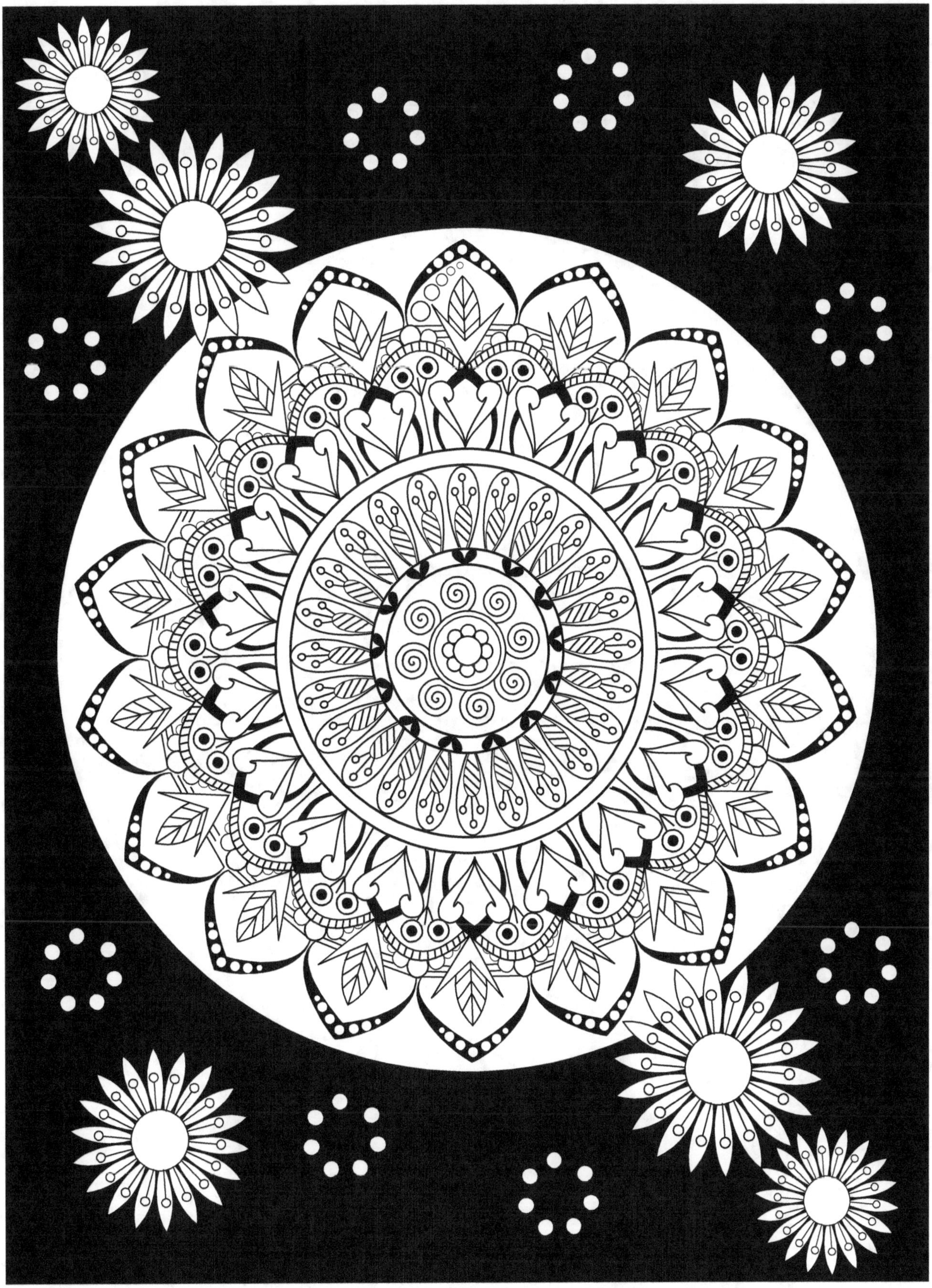

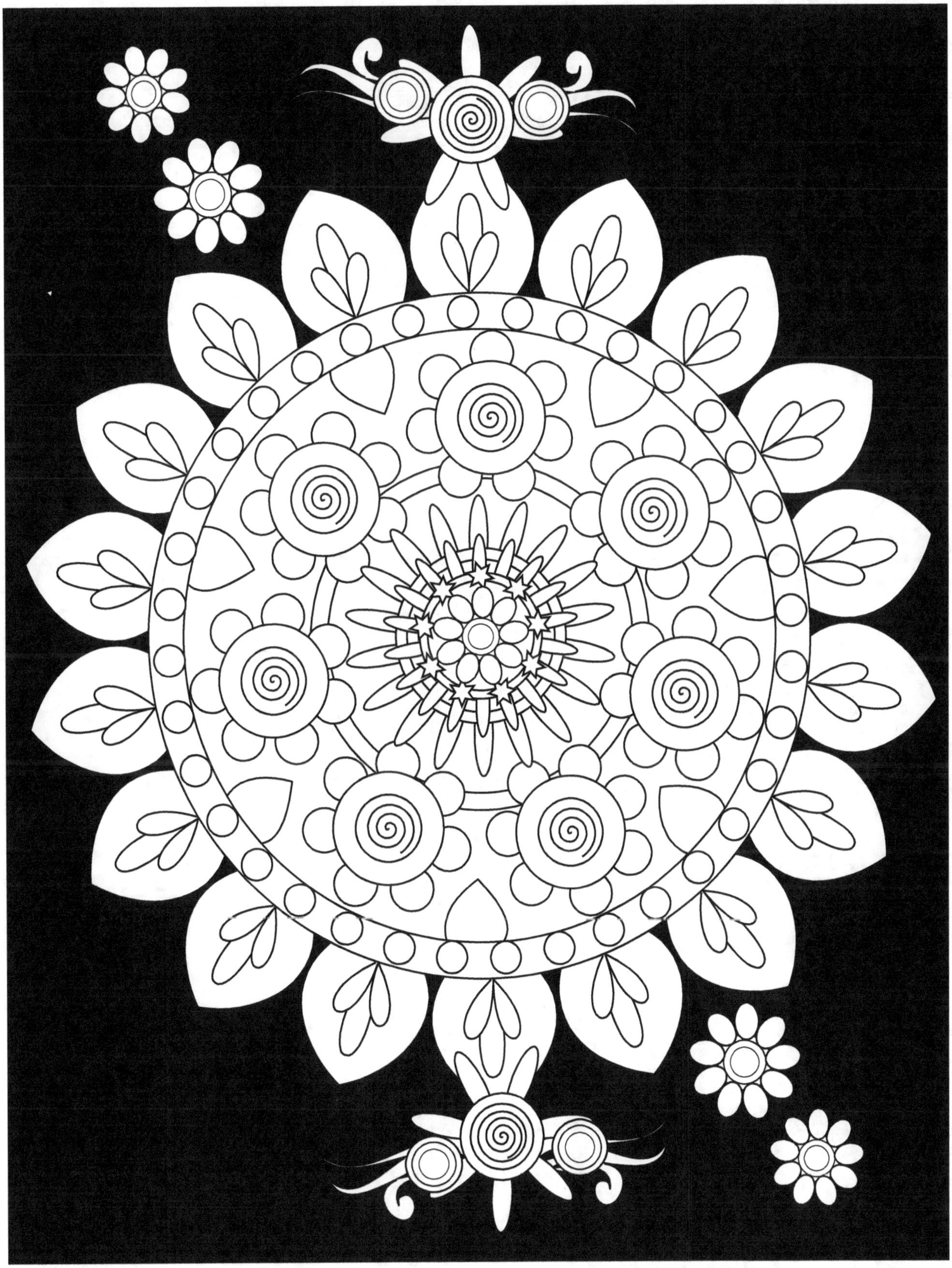

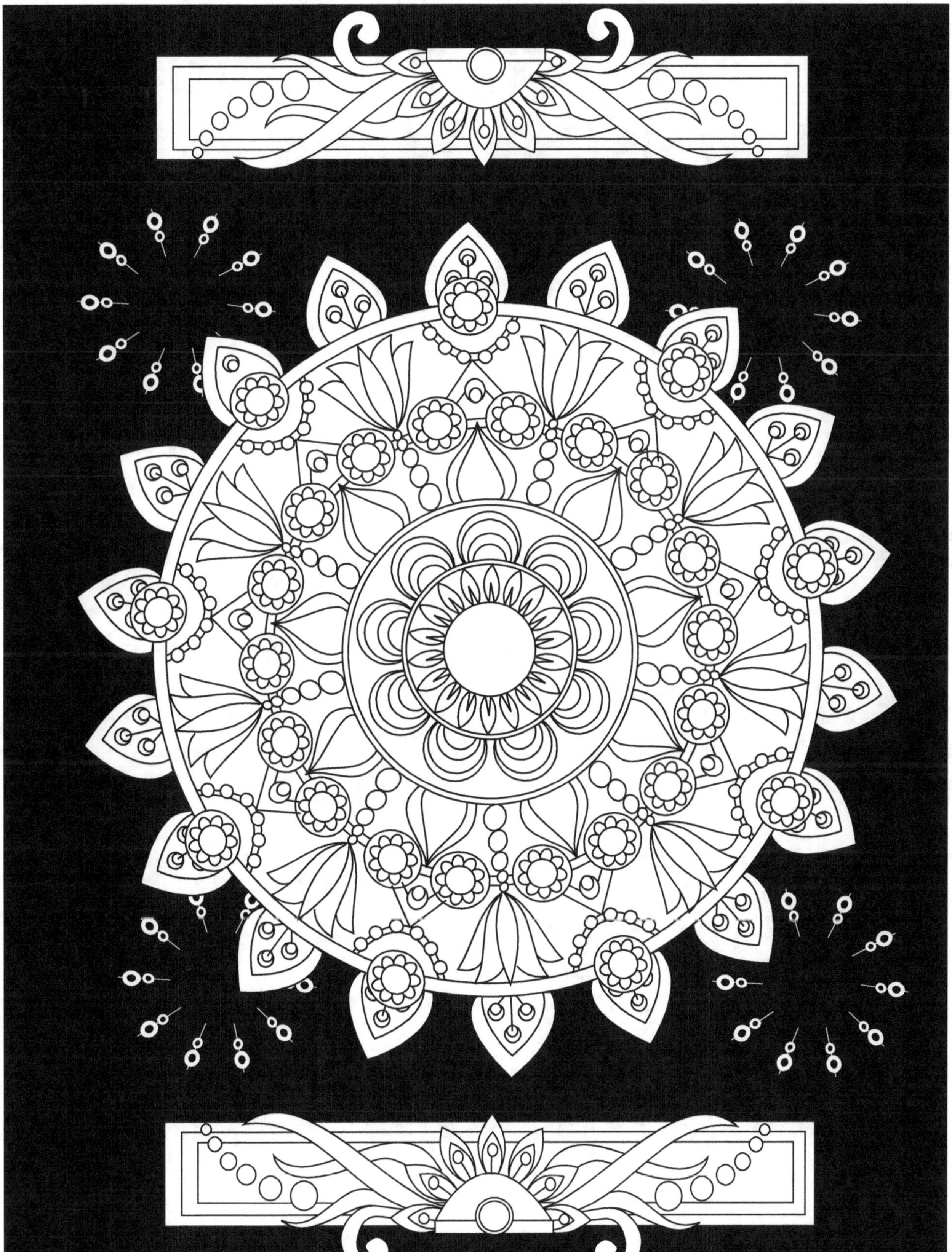

www.ingramcontent.com/pod-product-compliance
Lightning Source LLC
Chambersburg PA
CBHW062219220526
45471CB00009B/3272
* 9 7 8 1 9 8 6 6 7 5 0 0 0 *